To
Hazel Sermstew

A few unknown
about Ashie

Maybe the
should stay
that way

Boundary
Layer
People

Immigration & Education -
America's Hopes for the Future

Pete

Viggo Pete Hansen Ph.D.

BOUNDARY LAYER PEOPLE

Immigration & Education -
America's Hope for the Future

Published by

Dreams & Hopes
1119 Akron Street, Suite 100
San Diego, California, 92106

In association with Gainsway Press, Fullerton, CA

ISBN 1-930807-04-X

Library of Congress Catalog Number - in process

Paper - inn process
Hard cover – in process

Printed in the United States of America

1st Printing

To Dixie – my wife and dearest friend

Special thanks to
Ebba Peterson (nee Sandahl), a true Askovian
whose encouragement was paramount in completing
this story,
And to
Carol Gaskin, for her patience, tolerance and
outstanding editing skills.

2003 AD

Acknowledgements

I am not sure anyone really wants to be acknowledged or associated with what I have said about America's immigrants and our educational systems. Regardless, I thank you all – for charity and understanding.

Special thanks to -

- My immigrant parents, Emil Andreas Hansen, Gudrun Marianne Paulsen, who made it all happen, and to my doting and loving sisters; Solveig, Edith and their families.
- Erstwhile Danish Vikings for providing a relatively healthy gene pool and a sometimes-sick sense of humor.
- The intrepid Askovians, who have graciously survived rocks, rutabagas, and mosquitoes and gave me roots.
- My immediate and extended family who have kept me alive with their love, encouragement, ideas and challenges. To Alex, Anne, Debra, Erich, Ian, John, Kathy, Leesa, Mark, Paul, Pieter and those to follow - There is absolutely nothing like a loving and supportive family.
- All my students who for over a half-century toler-

ated and suffered my teaching. I surely learned more from you than you ever learned from me.

- Professional gurus and mentors; Johannes Knudsen, Ralph Redick, Donovan Johnson, Clarence Olander, Doyal Nelson, Tony La Bue, James O'Donnell, Joyce Feucht-Haviar, Bob Brocklehurst, to name a few.
- Colleagues worldwide, who generously gave of themselves to help me learn, survive and appreciate the importance of global education.
- My most precious thank you is to Dixie, my wife and companion who lovingly (I think) endures my idiosyncrasies. Without her support and encouragement this story would not have been told.

I wish that every one of you might be as lucky as I have been. –

Thank you all -

Contents

Introduction

FACT: The 2000 census indicated that one in five U.S. residents was born in another country or is a first-generation child born to new arrivals.

FACT: Americans love slogans.

Throughout our history we Americans have tried to stir up national patriotism to save our collective behinds by admonishing ourselves to remember: The Alamo, The Maine, Pearl Harbor, and recently, 9-11. But why-oh-why, given these great reminder slogans, do nasty events keep recurring?

The problem is certainly not that Americans have poor memories. No, our memories are dutifully at work as nature intended. The two reasons we have failed to mature from these costly and devastating events can be stated very simply.

1. Learning from our experiences requires hard work, cooperative efforts, diligence, and critical, emotion-free analysis of the events being studied. Hence it is much easier to let them slide into oblivion and hope to hell they never happen

again.

2. Lessons learned should lead to appropriate action based on the acquired knowledge. This is truly hard work and often costly, so we also pass on it, hoping things will somehow work out. Hope, of course, springs eternal, but often it fails to produce desirable results.

A decade ago I became somewhat guilt ridden by the realization that the children of America's immigrants, of which I am one, while having been extremely fortunate, have as a group failed to recognize and acknowledge their lucky fate, and that perhaps this oversight, though not intentional, has contributed to some horrific events throughout American history.

The 9/11 barbaric attacks on America forces us all to re-examine the last century in light of our immigrants and the manner in which Americans have become insular and even selfish at the expense of many less fortunate throughout the world. Our tendency to beat our chests and cry foul needs some study.

In the tribal cultures of old, the elders were responsible for passing on whatever knowledge their years had bestowed upon them. After decades of being lucky, it is time for those of us who are surely elders to share with others lessons learned from a bountiful past. Furthermore, these experiences may humbly suggest a course of action for America's future

The best way to attain the objectives of learning from the past and applying that wisdom to appropriate future action is via America's fantastic educational system(s). My most humble and modest suggestions are garnered from a lifetime of experience as a first generation American, an extremely fortunate group I call the

"Boundary Layer People." There are now lots of us - one in five - 20 per cent.

In modern physics, the term *"boundary layer"* refers to the molecular activity that takes place when the surfaces of two different materials rub against one another. As the hull of a boat plows through the water, a thin "boundary layer" of molecular activity between the hull and the water allows these two types of matter to adapt to and accommodate one another. The boundary layer molecules are a mixture - part hull and part water.

Likewise, I contend that the children of America's immigrants form a boundary layer of people, a generation who make the adaptations from a foreign culture to the ever-evolving America culture while embodying elements of both. Furthermore, it is essential for America's survival to maintain a constant inflow of immigrants, for it is in this thin human boundary layer that we find much of the incredible energy and creativity that is a constant source of renewal and growth in America.

As long as America continues to maintain a relatively open policy towards future immigration, this renewable source of creativity will continue to ensure America's leadership role in the world. But today we find that this openness and freedom is in jeopardy.

A second category of *"Boundary Layer People"* is America's professional educators. They dutifully serve in that boundary layer existing between students and their parents. It has been my good fortune to be involved in both.

Suddenly on September 11, 2001 my cozy reflections came crashing down as surreal video scenes showed the vaporizing of an American landmark in downtown New York, a city with a vast breadth of immigration experiences. Something had gone dreadfully wrong in America for it to be so brutally wounded. Was it our oversight, complacency, arrogance, laziness, ignorance, selfishness or, all of the above, that somehow stirred legions of "outsiders" to the American dream to explode in a rage of suicidal destruction and terror? Or was it simply frustrated envy gone awry?

Is America somehow responsible for the pain we now suffer?

Yes, in part, although certainly not intentionally.

Can we learn a lesson?   We must!

We must act expeditiously to determine the root causes of horrific events, before we end up compounding mistakes in our attempts to deter repeat incidents— or worse yet seek misdirected revenge.

Already a portion of blame is being directed toward our relatively open immigration policies. I hope to demonstrate the danger inherent in this knee-jerk criticism, and why any hasty curtailment of our immigration policies would be tragically counterproductive, as our immigrants are the wellspring for much of the vitality, ingenuity, and richness of American culture. Furthermore I assert that our only hope for dealing with future political catastrophes, including terrorism, is through better global education and a willingness to share our wealth with other, less fortunate earthly inhabitants.

Clearly most of the immigrants who have made America their home arrived relatively poor and hungry, and they have sought to improve their lot through hard work and frugality. But over the past few decades, the cleft between the haves and have-nots throughout the world has grown so insurmountable that it has spawned legions of bewildered souls who willingly take a path of self-destructive outrage—albeit with the promise of beautiful virgins awaiting their "crossing the bar".

Suicidal activity, conducted primarily by young people, is to the typical American simply abhorrent and downright crazy. It does not seem to fit any reasonable pattern—or does it? And how and why did religions get so enmeshed in these chaotic and destructive events? Most rationale people still subscribe to cause-and-effect relationships in things they view as being of a physical or economic nature. However, in philosophical or religious matter all bets are off. Suddenly an entirely new set of paradigms and behaviors emerges. Why?

We are now experiencing a phenomenal growth in the sciences. The reasons are simple, most scientists tend to share findings, openly examine gathered data and logically debate consequences. They have referees. Unfortunately in the social scheme of things we have an excess of folks who want you to believe they have an open conduit to their gods and are getting information that only they can handle, but by golly the rest of us had better believe them and follow. Much of this seemingly (miss) information dates back to times when records were few.

Mathematics and the sciences look for patterns that repeat and have a rational interpretation. This provides for uniformity and agreements. Sadly, even though there are strong common elements in humankind's many major religions, the emphasis is not on these similarities, but on the differences, because that is where you can make a game and generate an audience.

History and science both suggest there are reasons for every event. This means there is hope. But only if we first free ourselves from primitive unsubstantiated notions.

If that is the case, then we had better begin some serious soul-searching to uncover the causative problems in order to deter these unacceptable behaviors.

America was founded on the ideals of freedom and equality, and as such naturally attracts a variety of foreigners, good and bad, well meaning and opportunistic. Can we trace some relationship between the immigrants who succeeded in America and the folks who stayed home and progressed less rapidly or in a different direction? Has envy of America now become so intense that many will distort their belief systems by committing suicide in order to somehow, through twisted logic, "get even"? Where and how does this kind of threatening and illogical thinking begin?

How responsible is America for our present suffering?

More importantly, how can future tragedies be prevented?

Can we read the past to find the answers that will lead us into a safer and happier future?

In reviewing my experiences as an erstwhile and unfulfilled rutabaga farmer, a nuclear weapons officer, a public school and university teacher and administrator, a mathematics textbook author, and a consultant at large, I am reminded that every learner, young or old, farm boy or city slicker, does gain some knowledge by being educated. However, learners who are endowed with a good educational support system gain at a much faster rate, ultimately producing a gulf between the top and lower echelons. Inevitably the gap widens with time, providing the less fortunate with opportunities for envy and desires for aberrant behavior.

Consequently, frustration sets in for many students who are at the lower levels of achievement. They begin devising new and often deviant social structures to help them cope. Pent up negative energy sours to hatred and seeks to be released. This process appears to work the same way for individuals as for the poor versus wealthy nations.

As formal education has come under scrutiny, American schools have now embarked upon a completely desperate and off-the-wall program of "high stakes" testing. "Entitlement" has become a sacrosanct expression, along with the daffy notion of "political correctness". These concepts make it difficulty to openly discuss sensitive topics, which may harbor serious consequences, with our children, among ourselves, and among nations, for fear of offending. As a result we retreated to non-issues and meaningless measurements. What has become lost is a clear, honest reflection of our attitudes and how they influence the future.

Critical decisions are necessary and in making them we now need to consider the following - relatively new

- conditions.

• Knowledge is today almost free – thanks to technology. Only minimal skills are now needed to access this knowledge. A true revolution.

• Attitudes are extremely expensive and difficult to obtain. They develop over time.

• At issue today are global "high stakes" attitudes with potentially deadly consequences.

• Morality is an attitude - not an enforceable law. However it is the key to our survival.

In addition to squelching the concept of an examined life from our formal educational experiences, America is now also confronted by a malignant greed that is sweeping through our corporate leadership and threatens to severely damaging global economies. When people resort to selling their body parts to financially survive there is a major morality problem.

Problem: When too few have too much, too many have too little.

When we add to this volatile cauldron a highly restrictive and conservative self-appointed religious leadership component, horrific events can be anticipated, be they the bombing of abortion clinics, fancy nightclubs, pizza joints, or buses carrying students and workers. As these misguided and dysfunctional people become more enthused and absorbed with their vision of a rewarding life after their suicidal death, the prevailing world social structure, based on law and order, cannot long withstand the consequences.

To divert our minds from these topics, we gleefully embrace inane media productions and corporate sporting events. These diversions would be benign if we would also pay attention to the fundamentals necessary for humankind's long-term survival. Time is our most precious commodity; it must not be squandered.

Humankind must now create through its political, educational, social, economic, and religious structures procedures to identify when a situation is becoming unstable and to act accordingly, be it among nations or within the classroom.

Needed immediately:

Preemptive social remediation, including educational and attitude overhaul — not preemptive military strikes.

What were the conditions that allowed the 9/11 events to occur? The lack of communication within governmental agencies and loose immigration procedures were *not* the basic problems. The primary mischief-makers are found lurking in our educational and social philosophies and policies.

Our global problems are attitudinal!

America's intensive worldwide marketing strategies constantly encourage every one of us to get and consume more—of everything. We manufacture goods that are obsolete before they hit the marketplace. We have honed our marketing skills to such a feverish point that many are incapable of recognizing the sad truth that they cannot have everything being paraded as essential. Those who cannot afford these "essential" new things, but nonetheless have obsessive desires to get them, will experience stress and frustrations that often lead to crime and violence in both the private and corporate worlds.

The consumption frenzy is now global; but the planet cannot sustain it.

Avarice and criminal behavior on a local level are somewhat manageable and can be reckoned with, but now the stakes have become monumental as well as worldwide. This completely alters the equation, with a concomitant urgency for a solution that is fair and deters future abuses.

America, thanks to its immigration policies, has become rich and powerful. We have been generous to a degree, but at times also isolationist and self-indulgent, neglecting to help the multitude of less fortunate citizens and nations. It would appear that recently America has again drifted into a self-centered complacency that leads us to behave vengefully whenever our comfortable lifestyle is challenged.

In one short century America has gone from a rebellious upstart nation to the world's single superpower. American abundance of wealth is beyond belief. Unfortunately for far too many, so is poverty and inequity. This is definitely not what most immigrants had in mind as they built America.

While America was becoming ever more powerful, did we fail to recognize that our blue planet earth is indeed Buckminister Fuller's little space ship whereon every person and parts thereof interact? There are no more islands of isolation for America to hide in: we are crewmembers on the same vessel.

Today we see our space scientists, through international cooperative efforts, beginning to conquer space, however our social scientists seem ineffective in improving cooperative efforts here on earth. American society has not yet been able to elect and educate its political leaders to the same degree of cooperation the scientists have. Why?

Unfettered prejudice, inflated egos and lack of education come to mind.

We all create our own reality. For some it is hard work, music, or play. But for too many others, reality is confusion laced with frustrations. Whatever we perceive as our reality comes to define our being. Conversely, others' perception of our reality is distorted by their perception of their own reality. Around and around we go. We do have a choice. We can tighten this knot till it chokes all of humankind, or we can jointly try to slowly unravel the kinks through better education.

The challenge for each of us becomes to define our own reality through introspection, patience, and tolerance so as to peacefully accommodate the norms and standards of others. This is exactly what the American immigrants have done. Labeling others the "Axis of evil" is sure as hell not the way to stabilize nations and individuals who feel aggrieved.

We now have a zealous movement spreading across the land, touting a mantra of "We will never forget."

But the real issue has nothing to do with memory

and should rather be: "Have we learned anything?"
The answer is certainly not yet obvious.

Preservation of our species on this planet can only
come through global education and social services, both
of which are now readily available and relatively inexpensive, compared to violent measures. With this statement, it now becomes my challenge to define what kind
of education is required and to demonstrate ways for
us to accomplish these noble tasks.

We begin this journey by recognizing that mass
suicide, as has now befallen us, is the ultimate expression of human desperation and societal breakdown,
especially when the perpetrators justify their behavior
in the name of some perceived deity.

Let us also concede the fact that America can no
longer go it alone—we must have allies. To improve on
this deplorable state of global affairs, we need rational
thought coupled with humility and the abandonment
of national arrogance. Let us retire our narrow slogans
that often destabilize good common sense and instead
reach out to everyone.

As a rutabaga farmer might say, it is a long haul
lying before us, and its success will depend mightily
upon America's resolve and rely heavily on our educational establishments. The times are now truly global
and thus require global solutions.

Our immigrants, with their attitudes, perspectives,
and contributions, are America's greatest assets: they
bring the global issues to our shores. Boundary layer
people inherit the responsibilities of the assimilation
process. Many also become teachers, and I venture to

propose that future leadership for a peaceful and prosperous world will come from teachers across the globe.

Education has always been a primary concern of the immigrants. They instinctively know this is the future.

Our state tax-supported universities have become leaders in every field of knowledge. Early on I was fortunate to have accepted professional education as a career objective. To be associated with education for decades has been an unbelievably rewarding experience. I hope to demonstrate that it is American education that has become the hope for global human survival.

Perspectives on immigrants range from, "We must keep them out at all costs" to a more moderate position as to how we might develop new policies and procedures for admitting and perhaps monitoring them. Do they cost jobs for existing citizens or do they create them? Do they enrich or degrade our traditions, language, and culture? If and when they become voting citizens, which party do they gravitate to, and why? How may this alter the political balance?

The purpose of this book is to demonstrate and hopefully convince Americans that we must not fear our immigrants, but rather embrace them—they are our primary source of constant renewal for the future. The sum of America's parts (the immigrants) is greater than one.

With your indulgence, using limited and biased examples from my own boundary-layer life, I will try to make a case for America to remain the "Land of Immigrants".

I have borrowed the analogy of the boundary layer to illustrate how our First Generation Americans have traditionally formed an edge that mediates between the world of their parents and the established culture. Just as the hard edges between things turn out to be blurred on a molecular level, beginnings are often poorly defined. So I will be taking some literary license in discussing how Danish Vikings might have made it to a place in Minnesota they were to call Askov, named after a burg in Jutland, Denmark. I have at times sacrificed historical accuracy to ensure that readers will not be bored or confused. No test is scheduled at the end.

One last caveat: in spite of adversity, most Viking immigrants and their first generation kids in America had fun. These immigrants looked upon their travels as an adventure, and once they arrived in America there was no going back. Too often they had only their frivolity available to help them cope with their plight. I hope to capture a bit of that spirit in telling this story. The Danish Vikings were quite noted for their wry sense of humor, and their ability to trifle with the absurd and not take themselves too seriously.

This book is **NOT** about statistics. It is organized around three human perspectives:

• **A look at immigrants to America, how their traits influence and mold our nation, and why we must NOT fear immigration.**

• **Reflections on why reforming American education is absolutely critical to insure a peaceful—global— future for everyone.**

• **Personal experiences as a boundary layer person who was fortunate to have participated in educational "ventures".**

Each chapter offers a "lesson learned" as a closing statement. My intent is to summarize what a given period of time or specific events taught me. We seek closure, and often closing statements are simple – they say it all. Like the Viking salute -

Skoal!

Chapter 1
When & Who?

Time . . . the most ubiquitous concept in the human lexicon. We have difficultly measuring it; sometimes it seems to pass quickly without leaving a mark, while other times it seems interminably long and leaves deep scars. A child anticipating a birthday party has a different time frame of reference than a senior citizen playing cards in a nursing home. We use time to determine when certain events should occur—holidays, when we can get a drivers license. Time is exchanged for money. It poignantly marks most tombstones.

Most beginnings are tied to a statement about time, e.g., "the Atomic Age began in the twentieth century." The physicist often uses time (t) as a measure of distance (d) when pegging the beginning of our universe. Here the relationship is on how far light travels (where the speed of light is considered a constant) over a certain period of time—as in light years.

Science has today evolved into using nano-seconds (a millionth of a millimeter) where we are confronted with challenges, opportunities and concerns about devices that use individual atoms or molecules as components. The possibilities are staggering.

But even as we use the concept of time for daily chores, many people remain uncomfortable with it. Is time, as some suggest, a silent river flowing relentlessly in one direction only? Astronomers are on to something they call "wormholes," where the possibilities concerning time become staggering. In the shadowy realm of antimatter and black holes, does time perhaps run backwards?

Since time is seemingly so elusive, does it even exist? Philosophers, scientists, and ordinary folks have repeatedly asked this provocative and disturbing question. But those who question the existence of time, other than as we have codified it for practical use, are faced with the daunting task of explaining the passage of events. Time is indeed best defined by a big question mark. The manner in which we often talk about time is perhaps indicative of humankind's ultimate hubris.

Ever since humans developed an insatiable desire to know "when" something happened, we have been saddled with imprecise measures. Science informs us that we will never be able to know *exactly* when something happens. An earth year is a fuzzy measurement; in that a year is the "time" it takes our planet to whip once around the sun. Since this process is slowing down, the exactness is changing all the "time". Decaying atoms also have some limitations when used as a measuring instrument. Discussions about time and its units of measure are fascinating—especially in a bar later in the evening.

Our time scale now suggests that Europeans sloshed ashore in the Northern Hemisphere more or less a thousand years ago. These adventuresome Vikings encountered other folks, the Native Americans, who had been here much longer. (Just when the Native Americans got here and where they came from is still under investigation—government grants, you know.)

The early European immigrations to the New World were initially few and far between, with only archeological records testifying to the events. As these strangers from separate continents looked each other in the eyes, recognizing human similarities and yet unable to communicate, what were their feelings? These initial contacts between cultures—learning about each other's food, clothing, lifestyle, and beliefs—must have been exciting. We will not have that experience again until we meet entities from other planets.

As the stream of immigrants, legal and illegal, steadily increased, America quietly arose to its current superpower position. From the very beginning, and regardless of when and from what country the immigrants came, the first generation Americans have been and are a unique stratum in America's culture.

These first generations, boundary layer people, are significantly different from their compatriots, regardless of when and where they came from. European immigrants who were unhappy at home and wished to make a substantive lifestyle change initially founded much of contemporary America. There were other restless souls who periodically got into leaky, rat-infested boats and left Europe, Africa, Asia, and their ancestors forever, with only a dream and a hope, to come to America, a relatively unknown country. What was it that drove them to nourish this dream and then follow it up with action?

Today immigrants still come, braving the scorching and freezing climates of America's borders, on foot or in broken-down vans, as illegal cargo on foreign boats, and on 747s via state-of-the-art airports.

Thankfully we still have a virtual flood of immigrants coming from all the world's nations, rich and poor, through a wide variety of schemes, both legal and illegal. But no matter how and when they get to America, a newcomer's first expression was and continues to be, "Wow! We are finally in America and can feel, smell, and taste its intoxicating freedom. Now we will gratefully get to work to fulfill our dream." Immigrants did not, and for the most part still do not, seek entitlement; they just seek equality and the opportunity to work and earn a living in a free environment.

Many American citizens are concerned by this influx of gleeful foreigners. The exuberance expressed by newly arrived immigrants is often looked upon with jaundiced skepticism by the older and established citizenry. Is this immigration enthusiasm bad for America? I suggest the truth is quite the opposite. The newness of coming to America, with its hope, variety, and vast potential, begets this enthusiasm. Sadly this is often lost on future generations.

Immigrants of the past and present possess some very special traits that helped them get to America. These features are worth noting, because these are the very characteristics that have defined America as "the 'can-do' nation". Citizens of other nations who wish to come and live permanently in America face serious obstacles before leaving their native home, as well as on arrival. The fact that they succeeded renders them heroes in America as well as in their former homeland.

Just who are the people who become America's immigrants?

- They are positive, proactive people. They tend to have been deeply dissatisfied with their home conditions and their perceived future if they remained. They did not wallow in this unhappiness; instead they decided to do something positive.

- They are courageous and adventurous, willing to face unknown challenges, hardships, and even dangers to make a new life in a new land.

- They are "can-do" fighters who do not shrink from struggle. After making and surviving "the trip", all other challenges pale. Go to the moon and planets, conquer diseases, fight discrimination, win wars, feed hungry nations— all now viewed as doable.

- They are hardworking. Whether tilling land or opening a vegetable market, immigrants tend to work long hours to make their dream of a better life a reality for themselves and their families.

- They are extremely resourceful. The women prepare gourmet meals from things you don't even want to know. The men creatively construct buildings from every kind of local material. The children participate in daily chores essential for survival.

- They are not wasteful; every possession is dear and meaningful. At times this can lead to a pack-rat mentality.

- Humor sustains them. Even though they were un-happy at home, most possess an incredible sense of humor—look at some of our great comedians.

- They are coldly objective in assessing their situation, resulting in many attorneys and scientists.

- They are probably above average in intelligence. (This can't be measured, so is an educated guess.)

- They respect knowledge and seek to become edu-cated. Schools and discipline have been immigrant hallmarks.

- They are able to focus. They work single-mindedly toward their goals.

- They are flexible, willing to accept major and perma-nent changes. One result is that Americans move around a lot. We built interstate highways to facili-tate this desire.

- They are willing to accept extreme sacrifices for their ideals, including loss of life—even their own and fam-ily members'.

- They tend to be poor; indeed, many are desperate. This translates into an appreciation and humility for any subsequent wealth gained.

- They tend to be generous and to help those they left behind. Once established, immigrants typically send support back home and/or try to aid family mem-bers who also want to immigrate.

- They are willing to sublimate their native culture, in-cluding its political, social, and religious orientations for a new order. Here is where the boundary layer people are most effective.

- They believe fervently in the need for education as a key to a better life for their children.

- They are great gamblers, accepting the fact that they had little to lose at home, and betting it all that future odds in America will be in their favor. It is no won-der we have Las Vegas and a nation saturated with casinos.

- They invest all they have on a one-way trip. Unless they are illegal, get caught, and are shipped back, they tend to stay.

- They willingly tolerate a mountain of paperwork, bureaucracy, and hostile rejections after getting "in" and having to establish themselves.

- In most cases, they must also learn a new language—English.

- They cooperate. Some quietly form cooperatives and credit unions to facilitate sharing.

- They must constantly accept beginning anew. Every day brings with it a welcomed stream of fresh chal-lenges.

- They never seem to age. As their years pile up, they seemingly remain youthful and optimistic.

- Their glasses are always half full.

- *Most importantly – they have dreams and hopes.*

Through assimilation immigrants to America have been collectively passing on strengths and especially attitudes that have shaped America's future for generations. We can see some sort of "selection process" at work in the people who dare to become immigrants. The willingness and ability to accept risks has been paramount in giving America our current incredible global edge. Our "can do" attitude did not emerge from individuals who wished to simply "hang on" or "hang out". Hunkering down is always a flawed strategy. Standing still is at best going backwards. But with comfort comes complacency. Therefore, the status quo attitude, which surfaces with some regularity in America, must continually be challenged or it will metastasize like a debilitating cancer. The best way to counter a status quo attitude is by encouraging a population stream composed of energetic, proactive, visionary individuals—the nation's immigrants.

Arrogantly flaunting our prowess, as we seem to be doing, is counterproductive and may invite future disasters.

Carry a big stick but with great humility!

Daily we see arguments in the media about how immigrants are taking jobs from Americans and costing the taxpayer excessive monies to provide for support services, including education and medical assistance. We tend to ignore the facts that the tasks many immigrants perform are often at the very lowest level. Their crime, when it exists, is surely not at the Enron level, and few of the poor ever obtain major costly medical procedures. In truth, these immigrant people tend to do the jobs the rest of us shun, thereby helping to keep the nation's frail infrastructure functioning at the basic level.

There have been many bumps in America's immigration policies, notably the Chinese Exclusion Act of 1882, when people from China were barred from naturalization. Unequal, some would say unfair, quotas have also been experienced, along with preferential treatment for skilled artisans and political refugees.

However when we study nations that do not encourage immigration or that have heavily restrictive immigration policies, we see that they inbreed and tend to stagnate. America was founded at a time of widespread grief and dissatisfaction, and this country offered huge areas of open land. Therefore it became natural for "risk takers" from every nation to come take a look. They did look, and they did come. They still look and still come. Hopefully the trend will continue, ad infinitum.

Let us not forget that America's incredibly brilliant Constitution was authored at a time when immigration was needed and encouraged. Our Constitution has been the map and compass that offers immigrants guidance and hope through their process of being assimilated. It is this dream to which all human beings aspire.

The question about how long immigration can continue at its present level is moot, because we often overlook the number of second-, third-, or later-generation Americans who are now returning to the lands of their forebears, bringing back to these nations what they learned in America.

While immigration is unquestionably the vitalizing and beneficial lifeblood of America, we must also remain aware of the troublesome traits we all may have inherited from our immigrant forebears.

• We are witnessing many poor and homeless people who seemingly wish to live unfettered on the streets of our cities. These are individuals who generally have lost almost everything, resulting in depression and a sense of hopelessness. Many suffer from serious mental illness. However, they still crave that sense of personal freedom brought to America by the immigrants.

• As Americans age many stubbornly cling to an attitude of independence they acquired through time, the quality that reflects the very characteristics that got immigrants to America.

• America's work ethic, thanks to our tireless ancestors, is such that the average American now works 350 hours more per year than our counterparts in Europe. Two family incomes, or more, have become the norm. On average we Americans get approximately 13 days of vacation, while 26% of the work force gets none. Most Europeans get a month off and Japanese get 18 days of annual paid leave. Our intensive work schedules take time from rest, recreation, family, and physical activities, and encourage fast-food eating habits. Americans stressed for leisure opportunities do sacrifice time to adequately study politics and vote. This is a major challenge to a democracy.

America has developed incredible industrial capacity. The real and troublesome concern is the excessive consumption and selfish greed that has crept into our evolving culture. We are becoming bimodal, with too many who have too little, and a few who have too much—and herein lies the conundrum.

What follows next is my personal accounting of what happened to one American immigrant's kid, and how this boundary layer person's point of view developed as a result of those influences.

My parents seemingly possessed most of the above-listed characteristics as immigrants to America. I became one of the lucky boundary layer recipients and experienced firsthand how fortunate we, their kids, were. Using anecdotal accounts, some tragic, some comic, I will try to reconstruct and share vignettes from a Danish immigrant family living in a mostly immigrant community during a period of many wars, a depression, and unimaginable technological advances.

The background setting will be Scandinavian, specifically Danish, but every other ethnic group of immigrants to America has comparable tales to tell. Each of the many varied cultural backgrounds has contributed in some measure to the American mosaic, which is redesigned on a daily basis.

Most of us lucky first generation folks have not, singly or collectively, expressed our appreciation and gratitude to our forebears, perhaps through oversight or simply because we have been too busy enjoying the largess they provided us. Sadly, and more importantly, we have not formally taken a strong positive position in American politics when it comes to immigration policies.

It is time for boundary layer people to reflect, give thanks, and encourage America to keep welcoming our immigrants. They have provided the nourishment and ideas to continually produce a healthy, vibrant, and ever-growing America. Additionally they provide ongoing insurance against America creating an indulgent, self-serving monolithic government. No other nation in the world has such a diversified set of representatives as America.

However we have recently entered a period of our history when some of these benevolent attributes are in danger of being tampered with.

- **Knowledge must prevail over ignorance, yes; but attitudes should dominate and guide us.**

- **Greed and avarice, ever present and pervasive, will continue to challenge our survival, but perhaps after recent events American society will, as has happened in Scandinavia, take steps to be more insightful and curb abuses.**

- **Aging, by individuals and nations, is perhaps a myth. Avenues of optimism that encourage continued growth and development must replace the sometimes-bumpy roads of longevity.**

  Lesson Learned:
  Pick your parents; try for immigrants.

Chapter 2
Fuzzy Beginnings

Beginnings are often fuzzy; things just seem to happen, but we have only loosely concocted notions of why, when, or how. Take the origin of the universe. It is widely reported a Big Bang occurred some time ago, but as yet we have only inferential data suggesting it really did happen. Typically we do not even care how something got started, except when we need to give credit or fix blame. After a bar brawl has begun, it is too late to worry about who threw the first punch—at least until the attorneys get involved.

The historical information available to inform this peek into the boundary layer Danish Americans and their importance to our nation is truly fuzzy. So we stir in a little humor, some spurious "facts", and accept the outcome with uncertainty—with a nod to Professor Werner Heisenberg.

In fact, there is data galore to back up who came when, where, and the like; but too much data simply roils the waters, and we tend to lose sight of the real human meaning of immigration. I did some modest research of articles and documents on the topic of American immigration. It simply strengthened my resolve to try to make a case for keeping our doors relatively open to everyone.

I dislike diaries and also, at times, the folks who compulsively keep them. Obviously I never kept a diary. A major problem with diaries is that they are generally too accurate. They usually contain too much specific, but useless information along with an intense emotional component of the moment—lessons President Nixon and his cronies learned the hard way. Another real drawback of a diary is that you are constrained in embellishing your experiences and memories. With detailed logs you are not permitted to selectively forget past embarrassments or to delete any documented stupid behavior. Political leaders often never learn this saw.

But the worst feature of a diary is you are limited in soaring with lofty thoughts and great "might have been" deeds, because your diary has your butt nailed to the floor. Lucky me, I am not tethered to a log, a journal, or a good memory. I suffer no compulsion to reveal past sticky situations. This is called highly selective reflection, or simply being smart about one's past. Thus in compiling this brief treatise on the importance of American immigrants, I have included just the facts and some fantasies as I remember or have modified them to make a point. I found this a damn simple technique, by which the author remains completely guiltless, as well as purposefully clueless.

America, as a relatively small piece of Planet Earth, is richly endowed with physical features that provide its inhabitants with a rich and varied assortment of vegetation, minerals, climate, and wildlife. It has both flat prairies and mountainous surfaces and a wide range of inhabitable climates. Physically, the Garden of Eden probably looks a lot like America, except without attorneys, religions, and political parties. As a periodic physical reality check, America does have tornadoes, hurricanes, and earthquakes, along with hot and frosty interludes—just enough activity to keep us on our toes. In general, most of the immigrants who came and come to America, from those we call Native Americans to the folks now arriving daily on our borders, shores, and airports, have been pretty good stewards of our land. Oh yes, there has been some bad stuff, largely perpetrated by excessively greedy land and energy barons, corporate executives, inept government stewards, SUV drivers, and the like. But in general physical America is today still the most desirable geographical place on earth to live; and if we put on rose-colored glasses, it seems to be getting better.

Dams now assist us in controlling our water supply, weather forecasts help us prepare for stormy weather, farming techniques ensure better crops, and genetic engineering improves our animal herds and plants. America is indeed, "O Beautiful, for spacious skies, for amber waves of grain." The enhancement of American real estate is largely the result of the "can do" immigrant attitudes.

The challenge now confronting America is how to assist all the residents of the planet to work harmoniously together to ensure we do not collectively succumb to a variety of pollutions, deforestations, violence, and uncontrolled population growth. Unluckily for us, complete destruction is now within our means.

A unique and fortunate feature of American immigrants has been their ability to work collectively, in spite of radical differences, to build a better America. Their unwavering objectives are freedom and opportunity, something every human is born with. This skill is now sorely needed on a global scale.

What is missing is a clear understanding of what the immigrants' kids, the boundary layer folks, are like, and why, in spite of being the lucky ones, they may have unintentionally contributed to our current horrific problems. In today's sometimes heated debates on immigration policies, it is important to show how significant various generations have been in shaping America's future. Perhaps most troubling is the observation that the beneficiaries of all this wealth, freedom, and opportunity have too often lacked the vision or fortitude to "share" adequately with the world at large.

"He who dies with the most toys wins." Anonymous, Capitalists' Motto. Alive and well in America.

First generations are the result of a series of unique circumstances that continually re-create and mold a new social and cultural arrangement that differs from that of their immigrant parents. First generations tend to be restless, active, outgoing, and to some extent tolerant of diverse behavior, much as were their parents.

First generations must learn to straddle two lifestyles in America. The first is the one at home, which reflects their parents' cultural origins and where the native language often dominates. The other component of this schizoid life is the ever-evolving culture existing outside the home, and for many includes learning a new language, English. To survive, first generations must adjust to and accommodate at least two different worlds; they live in a cultural boundary layer.

Immigrant parents brought and continue to bring historical baggage from their native lands. But as their American-born kids get exposed to this reservoir of the past, they quickly set out to modify it so it will be acceptable in their American environment. This breeds and fosters creativity for real-life problem solving—the two areas where America has succeeded brilliantly. It's no accident, therefore, that the traits of creativity and problem-solving ability have come to characterize American culture as a whole.

One specific example: Today, just as years ago, there are still large segments of the American population who speak a language other than English in their home and whose social order strives to retain some of their parents' past. California administers its driver's license in some fifty languages. A Chinese immigrant can take his driver's license test in Chinese, while his kids can take it in English, or maybe Spanish. This is incredible.

We are now adding acceptable words and expressions to our everyday vocabulary at a phenomenal pace, from rap music lyrics to technical acronyms. No other nation is able to do this; they simply copy and follow us. It is no wonder that many languages are now languishing, indeed disappearing, and this is truly sad, like losing a species. But in their place are arising many totally new expressions. As a multi-lingually enriched form of English becomes a world standard, our opportunities for global communications are improved.

In part thanks to the immigrants, the American English language has exploded and now incorporates many other forms of communication. Foreign words are gobbled up, new words are created, and pictographs often do the job faster than words, as visual media can convey much greater quantities of information to our brains. Pictures truly are worth thousands of words. (Though interestingly few Asian symbols have crept into America's daily written material.) Some research findings even suggest that bi- or multi-lingual children are better able to ignore misleading information. The ability to switch between languages may indeed also contribute significantly to many of the creative ideas generated the boundary layer people.

This language issue is not trivial.

It has, and still does, give rise to both tolerant and intolerant behaviors. But on the positive side, it provides cultural enrichment by incorporating new expressions with unique nuances and at the same time enhances communication efficiency that is provided by acronyms, logos, and bar codes. Where would NASA, the corporate world, or the education and medical professions be without acronyms?

Acronyms are like mathematical equations; a few carefully selected symbols express volumes of knowledge and experience. Frequently they also carry an emotional load. For example, ER denotes a hospital's emergency room, often a place of great stress. SST reminds us of very fast airliners.

More recently the use of Internet "chat rooms" have resulted in a wide range of symbol usage, often sloppy, that reflects changes in daily communication patterns. Words in these situations may be spelled differently—Tootsie 4 governor—mixing sounds and shapes in creative formats, with minimal attention to style or grammar.

First generations have been highly active in the language area, because they had to create a boundary language that would work with their parents at home and in their American school and community. Slang helped serve this need and has now become an acceptable communication tool, yet we often tend to denigrate it.

First generations have had to mold their future by accepting the challenges of a new order while simultaneously clinging to past mores for the sake of peace and solace in the family. They experience one set of acceptable standards on the home front and often an entirely different set of norms in school and at work. This is often troublesome for kids who are embarrassed by their parents' clothes, broken English, and the kinds of foods they prepare with their unique aromas.

The European immigrants who came to America up to the early 1900's were a vastly different bunch than those coming to America today. Thanks to the mass media, today's immigrants have a clearer view of the America they seek than did the earlier Europeans. Virtually all have experienced a variety of America's sights and sounds before coming here. Many have sung and danced to American music, enjoyed our ridiculous television programs, and seen too many of our violent movies before arrival. They know our sport heroes and movie stars. America's high-tech entertainment has perhaps had the greatest influence on immature and confused young minds. Here lurk dark shadows.

They have also seen depictions of America's great accomplishments, however—Apollo's moon landings, our outstanding medical achievements, and our capacity to generate wealth, at least for some. Nonetheless, immigrants all seem to reflect the same alluring message about American promise: Americans dream big, and we want to come and play in your sandbox of unfettered freedom.

America's immigration policies today have not changed appreciably from those one hundred years ago. This has been to America's advantage. We have undoubtedly seen outrageous abuses, but overall these policies must not be too bad to have assisted in creating this nation, to which most everyone now looks for leadership, and where many still desire to emigrate. Ongoing maintenance and improved record keeping is always appropriate, and it appears that some items are in need to repair, including the replacement of some administrators. But if our immigration policy isn't completely broken, let's not over-fix it.

What all immigrants had, and still have, in common is a humble wish and a deep desire to be free, to start something that is uniquely them and permit their thoughts to be expressed openly. Herein is generated that exciting fabric of creativity that defines America. It is most difficult to be creative in a restrictive society.

Frightening and extreme forces exist that would, on one hand, greatly curtail our freedoms, or on the other hand advocate anarchy. America's immigrants, many of whom came from cultures that were limiting and authoritarian, have often assisted in finding a balanced middle position between these extremes. Many of them have experienced these polarized positions at home, so they know first hand how destructive they can be. America must be grateful for their knowledge, appreciate their input, and recognize their skill to negotiate.

Most immigrants possess a strong desire to work, frequently for long hours at relatively low pay, thereby creating a political conundrum. Do immigrants really work harder and cheaper than other Americans? Perhaps. Nonetheless, they must be given fair and equal treatment to which all citizens are entitled; otherwise, these issues simply fester and create undue tensions. The paramount immigration concern should focus on the long-range effect they have on America, not simply today's fickle job market issues.

There is, for sure—for sure, plenty of work for everyone who is interested. Aren't we lucky? Work defines every human being.

One positive effect of hungry people wanting to work is that this population puts pressure on the rest to avoid becoming too complacent. Competition leads to a better America by engendering new ideas while simultaneously keeping all of us on our toes. The sports craze that in one way or another involves most of us is a natural extension of this competitive spirit.

But we need to limit competition as well; through our varied social agencies we need to create support systems for those who are incapable of surviving in a highly competitive atmosphere, be it school, work, or play. This issue, too, becomes political. Who deserves a boost and who does not?

Today's pervasive concept of entitlement certainly did not exist in the immigrant culture I grew up with. My family's ethic, simply put, was "You are entitled to something when you have earned it, and not before." Having said that, however, let us not overlook the fact that immigrants, yesterday and today, have also tended to put education and medical support services in place to ensure that no one would suffer and be left behind. It is no trick to soar with the eagles as long as your eyesight is sharp and both wings flutter properly; but for those with handicapped wings and bad eyes, a social support system is a must. Furthermore, many of the people who do receive assistance repay by making valuable and unique contributions.

Envision our planet as a borderless world. This would severely challenge both the intellectual and political incest that now exists in many lands. The need to save the planet's abundant, but limited; resources would truly become a global issue. Already, the challenges regarding fresh air and water are on the verge of becoming global, albeit very hot button, items. Our focus must now shift to dreams of improving the planet for everyone's enjoyment and survival. This is exactly what the immigrants attempted, and to a great extent succeeded in doing, for America. Our ability to share resources across state lines needs to be expanded to cross national boundaries.

Being a lucky boundary-layer American, it is with a sense of humility and gratitude that I will try to weave some personal experiences, based on a Scandinavian background, into a position paper that hopefully supports America's continued acceptance of new immigrants—from everywhere.

The following selectively recalled experiences extend from stories told by my immigrant parents, who to their very end maintained continuity with their past in Scandinavia, to our kids, where the immigrant's roots are now back two generations and are quickly and sadly being forgotten. However, this loss is not that serious, since our culture is continually being rejuvenated by other new first generations from other parts of the globe.

My purpose is twofold; first to enthusiastically support America's historic and generous immigration policies, by looking at the immigrants' contributions and how they were filtered through a boundary layer of people to create today's America and secondly what has been their impact on education.

Lesson Learned:

Boundary layer people creatively change America.

Emil Hansen with oxen used for "sodbusting" in Eastern Montans circa 1912.

Chapter 3
Askovian Viking
Rompings

Loosen up for a moment as we, in a whimsical way, lay a foundation as to how the first Danish Vikings might have arrived in the American Midwest. Hopefully this account reflects some of the fantasy and fables many of us were told as children . . . back in a time period before radios and television, when storytelling was used to entertain kids.

My favorite historian, R. G. Collingwood, wrote in his book *The Idea of History*,

History is a science of human action: what the historian puts before himself is things that men have done in the past, and these belong to a world of change, a world where things come to be and cease to be. Such things, according to the prevalent Greek metaphysical view, ought not to be knowable, and therefore history ought to be impossible.

This expresses exactly my sentiments about what follows. So please rest at ease regarding the issues of historical purity in what I have to say about Askovian

Viking rompings along the Great Kettle River many years ago. Imagine, if you will, a doting mother striving to entertain some rebellious kids while doing her chores. Just as she did not take her tale too seriously, neither should you. It is revisionist's history.

A long, long time ago, after the bitter cold periods of the various ice ages, there were some restless Danish Vikings who made forays into the new world long before other Europeans. They were adventurous, bored, and foolhardy, but also gutsy. Just when this took place we are not sure—but they were here long before the Italians. We do not know how many there were, but we do know they made wooden boats with squared sails that repeatedly took them far northwest from Scandinavia. Remnants of these boats have been found in several Northern locations.

One of these Viking armadas of quaint, but fierce-looking little wooden boats, driven by the frosty shifting winds around Greenland and Newfoundland, became accidentally separated from the larger group. The sagas tell us that the skies were clouded over for a long period of time, so they could not see Polaris, their guiding star. These Vikings sailors, probably in search of booze and broads, found its way into the St. Lawrence River and Great Lakes area, where they came quite by accident on Lake Superior. After landing they hiked to an area of North America that later became known as Minnesota, and it still is.

After many months of casting around aimlessly in their open boats on the cold and stormy Atlantic and the Great Lakes, we must assume that this land was a welcome sight for these travel-weary Vikings.

They had indeed arrived somewhere—but where?

The Danes who "made it over" discovered a land with boundless, beautifully green pine forests. Among the trees were pristine blue lakes and gently flowing rivers. The lakes were filled with all kinds of fish; some had no bones and were later called sturgeons, still the source of some of the world's best caviar. Like all new arrivals to anyplace, these early Viking discoverers immediately decided to get into the real estate game. We have all done this when we first visit a new place—ja, we must for sure buy a second home or at the very least get a time-share.

To this very day, lots of Danes are very enterprising, especially in Denmark. These early Vikings cleverly schemed to return to Denmark and sell parcels of land in what was later to become, first Partridge, then Askov, Minnesota. Their dreams of bags of *kroners* from projected land sales drove them silly with avarice. It is believed, although not documented, that right there and then in Askov, they invented Danish folk dancing to celebrate the occasion.

They say, if the truth were known, that this loosely structured hopping around that formally goes by the name of folk dancing is fundamentally a sobriety test. Anthropologists, who study these things, say that most cultures throughout history have developed a variety of *folklorico*, and you really do see it everywhere. Whenever we visit a new country I am always leery of getting too close to these performances, especially if I have had a drink or two.

Before taking to the seas again, the Danish Vikings engaged in pre-real estate sales partying in earnest. It is also suggested in the sagas that the explorers created a liquid mixture of wild berry juices, roots, and fungus, probably the earliest experimentation with *glogg*. In the summertime they danced and romped in the buff with nubile Ojibwa maidens along the Kettle River, a river that has nothing in common with the Amazon except nude swimming.

Additionally the newly choreographed Danish folk dances were creatively beefed up with more popular Brazilian *lambada* styles. This dance combination later became well known as the *"Kettle River Trot"* and resulted in rapid, almost uncontrolled population growth.

Observing these strange Viking behaviors, the peaceful native Ojibwa Indians in the area began consulting their elders and medicine men to see if the Danish Kettle River Trot was catching, and if so, was there a cure. Since no one was certain, the Kettle River Trot effectively kept the Vikings safe from Ojibwa Indian attacks.

At this local Askovian riverbank encampment, the Viking population grew and flourished while their dreams of returning to Denmark to sell real estate were shelved as the merriment continued unabated. Life was good. But then, by golly, one day it started to cool off, and it just kept getting colder and colder. Temperatures plummeted, snow fell, and finally the lakes and sturgeons with their caviar-laden bellies froze. The frolicking Danes realized they again needed to make some kind of lifestyle adjustment to cope with this new situation. So it was back to Viking bearskin attire and crawling around underground to keep warm.

The Askovian countryside now sparkled crispy white with frozen blue lakes. After a long period of time that seemed like eons, these shivering Danish Vikings developed a mentally healthy attitude toward all this cold weather. After all, it reminded them of old Denmark, from when they had come. Inside their mostly underground dirt hovels, they made up wacky stories of *nisse,* or Danish gnomes, who were a kind of underground grump just like themselves, accept much smaller and more devious. Nisse constantly had to be placated with porridge or they would create mischief. Time passed while they sang and danced the Kettle River Trot, drinking glogg and making love. At length they began to realize that all these funny nisse stories they had concocted to cover their misery were getting tiresome and almost appeared to be stupid—which indeed they are.

A perspective: Denmark, a little spit of land jutting up from northern Germany, is surrounded by lots of little islands whose total population today is only five million people. The Danes have adapted well to their limited circumstances, which presumably reflects their intelligence quotient. No doubt they inherited this wonderful adapting ability from their ancestors who spent some time in cool Askov, Minnesota.

Not surprisingly some of the landlocked Askovian Viking vagabonds were again getting restless. They began musing about returning to their native Denmark after these many years away, recalling their earlier ideas of becoming rich realtors in Denmark. All Danes like to sell stuff. Take a walk down Stroget in Copenhagen today, and you'll see what I mean. Everything that is loose is for sale.

Though they were now living, or more accurately existing, underground in what we would call a semi-ice age, they kept remembering earlier times, when lush green fields reached to the horizon, and lakes and rivers teemed with sturgeons—a time before everything was under all this snow and ice. So they figured, hell, the folks back home in Denmark won't know the difference; we'll tell them what it was like here along the Askovian Kettle River before the big freeze. We will quickly close real estate sales, take the money, and sail off to somewhere else. (Escrow companies had not been invented due to a lack of competent lawyers—same problem as exists today.)

The issue was unanimously settled. They decided to get into their long neglected, funny-looking Viking boats and sail, this time eastward, through the Great Lakes, across the Atlantic Ocean, to home. Off they went, smoking their pipes and merrily singing folk drinking songs as the cold gusty winds blew them back to good old Denmark. They probably bounced off of Greenland and Iceland on their homeward-bound trek.

Ja-hoo, another adventure.

Some of the lucky returning Danes made it home, while of course the unlucky ones didn't. But big disappointments faced them on their return, because very few local Danes had any interest in their Viking real estate scam. Sadly these tired old crusty sailors, who had dreamed so greedily of selling Askovian property, instead had to settle into raising pigs and eating open-faced sandwiches like other stay-at-home farming Danes. How humiliating.

Hard as they all tried, though, these once-adventuresome Vikings could not forget their earlier rowdy exploits along the banks of the Kettle River. It is, of course, not well documented, but this may have been the beginning of the saying "melancholy Danes," which was used then to describe the demeanor of these former valiant explorers. Now the expression has been given wider application, thanks to bad media.

These mournful vagabonds would, every evening, as well as early in the morning and throughout the day, sit along the dusty cow paths in Jutland, drinking lukewarm Carlsberg beer while recalling stories of long ago. Initially their ludicrous tales had the status of male bovine droppings, but with time and endless embellishments these stories earned the sacrosanct status of sagas. There you have it.

Guess what?

The offspring of these early Ice Age marauders started having dreams of their own based on the fabricated sagas told by their forefathers. They, too, now desired to set sail to the Askovian green fields and lakes full of sturgeons they had heard about, not to mention the congregating with nubile ladies along the Kettle River after dancing the legendary trot. At length a groundswell of new Vikings explorers arose. For those of you in today's marketing business, the moral learned by these Danes is that you cannot always tell how long it will take for your inflated story to bear fruit. Marketing is everything, but timing is tricky.

When the old, tired would-be entrepreneurs, the former seafaring Danes, saw this emerging trend among their youth, it reawakened their desire to get kroners out of them—fast. They renewed their tale-telling with gusto, selling land – sight unseen—to their fellow Viking dreamers who had made lots of money raising pigs.

As you probably did not know, but will now, Danish pigs have an extra rib, making for extra cash. This is true.

Finally, another bunch of Danish Vikings headed west in their strange open boats with a single sail. But they were not lost; they were guided by the tales of old. In their hands they tightly clasped the land deeds they had purchased to this Garden of Eden called Askov. They were convinced they would become the nouveau riche property moguls that the sagas had foretold.

"Ja, sure, it vestvard ho ve go," they chanted, in Danish of course.

On the other hand the old salts, the sellers of these bogus land deeds to a generation of gullible dumb Danes, could not believe their good fortune. They hastily stuffed their newly gotten kroners in wooden casks and headed off to the Virgin Islands, again seeking booze and broads, but this time in a better climate and with more money.

Wouldn't you know it? They succeeded for a second time. This time these has-been Askovian Vikings founded the Virgin Islands. You really have to wonder how they decided to give these Caribbean Islands that name. It is not particularly Danish in origin or sentiment.

Now up north, activity was ramping up as the Great Danish Migration to Minnesota was about to begin. Ja, hoo, it vas velly cool. Winter was about over, but the land was still covered with snow.

It is reported that when the Ojibwa chief first spotted this returning ragtag nutty band of Vikings he hastily called his elders together. It had been many, many years since the former Viking group had left the Kettle River, and the Indians had assumed they would never be plagued by them again. But no way, here they came, merrily singing their killer folk songs. There was, however, a major difference this time: the Vikings had brought women with them.

"Oh my, what to do?" the chief wondered aloud,

all the while puffing rapidly and deeply on his beautiful long-stemmed pipestone pipe. (These pipes are made from pipestone found only in Pipestone, Minnesota, and that is why they are called Pipestone pipes.)

An ominous quiet arose among the Ojibwas as they began to realize a major calamity was about to befall them. With an eerie sense of déjà vu, these peace loving people began to recall their forefathers' earlier encounter with these mentally and physically "lost at sea" Vikings.

"Is it going to happen again?" They shuddered as the air is filled with tension.

"Quickly! Gather our medicine men and anyone else who can think outside the teepee so we can make a plan!" yelled the nervous chief. "We must be prepared. This is much worse than a Minnesota blizzard!"

Cautiously, Viking buddies Sven and Olaf, who did not look or smell too swift after sailing for many months, swaggered up to the Ojibwa chief and his hastily convened council with their water-soaked bogus deeds to Askovian property.

"Vee is here to claim oor proportee," said Sven, as he handed over the soggy documents to the chief's trembling hand. The chief maintained his composure, wondering what in the world this nut was up to.

The Ojibwa elders with great aplomb nodded knowingly and suggested that they all sit in a circle and discuss these property matters properly. These wise elders had a hard time not bursting out in laughter as the Viking sitting circle was being formed. These Vikings were not used to sitting cross-legged in a circle, and for sure not on frozen snow and ice.

"Great idea, chief," said Sven, and he hurried off to get some aquavit to facilitate the discussions. Sven was a take-charge kind of guy. Furthermore he needed a drink.

The chief fiddled with his beautiful long pipestone pipe, which excited Olaf, because he, too, liked smoking—a habit that all well bred, and not so well bred, Vikings pick up in their pre-teen years.

The Ojibwa leadership was completely dumbfounded that anyone would want to legally lay claim to the notorious Askovian rock pile. *There must be a trick in the making,* was the Chief's assessment. *Be wary.*

Around this roaring Kettle River campfire, with a full golden moon above and howling coyotes in the pinewoods, the Ojibwa and Viking male leaders, sitting on ice, began the task of establishing a working relationship regarding Askovian property rights. The wise medicine men became convinced that the now lubricated, hang-loose Danes were not an immediate threat to Ojibwa health and welfare, and they for sure had good tasting aquavit. Things might just work out all around.

Olaf, however, was fidgeting and beginning to show his frustrations at not yet having gotten a drag off the chief's beautiful pipestone pipe. "Chief, may I please try your pipe?" he blurted. Olaf was not at all interested in the fine points of land politics at that moment; he just needed a hit off the Chief's pipe. It looked and smelled so good.

The cagey chief knew it was too early in these delicate negotiations to allow the Vikings to smoke his precious pipe, which was filled with dried dandelion greens and other special ingredients. He inhaled a long, deep, teasing drag, then let out a stream of smoke as he calmly explained to Olaf, "You, dear Viking nomad, may have a puff as soon as we solve the legal problems you guys brought with these bogus Danish property deeds, and not before. Is that clearly understood?"

"Oh, ja, for sure, chief," replied Olaf, showing considerable embarrassment at his own impatience. "Ve vill vait oor turn."

The chief went on to explain that the documents were not worth the wet paper they were written on, and that furthermore, none of his intelligentsia could read the funny Danish alphabet. It had too many letters. (The Danish alphabet does have extra letters, you now know.)

"Hmmm." Sven took another fast swig of aquavit and came up with a clever solution. "Let us trow da damn tings in da fire to see if they vil burn."

"Clever idea," agreed the beaming chief, nodding to the elders, but careful to not display too much pleasure—or burst out laughing.

Into the fire they went, where they spit and sputtered all night long because they were soaked with salt water. By morning they would be simply glowing embers.

The Ojibwa and Viking males now fetched their wives and girlfriends, and with loud whooping and hollering, again joyously begin the famous Kettle River Trot. In spite of the Vikings' not-so-stellar social reputation, this encounter with the Ojibwa in Askov was probably the most peaceful settlement ever made in North America. Everyone agreed on everything.

To this very day, the Danish language has lots of cryptic and meaningless expressions of unknown origin that probably came from Askov in those early years. It was a language born of necessity. I remember I learned many of these words and expressions as a child, but could never use them in the presence of adults. They were special sounds that could only be used in selected settings for special purposes.

It is also reported that it was at this time that the Scandinavian Boat System, SBS, was formed to assist in hauling Danish Vikings to Askov. SBS would later change its name to SAS, the Scandinavian Airline System, when airplanes became plentiful.

Finally the big thaw came to Askov, Minnesota.

Ja, for sure, vhat a surprise. another Great Askovian Ice Age had ended.

As the snow slowly turned to water and began filling the creeks, these Danish immigrants discovered that the ice ages had hauled and pushed ninety percent of all the rocks in the Northern Hemisphere to Askov. Another nine percent of the rocks were deposited in Sandstone, a scant eight miles to the south of Askov. The final one percent of boulders were scattered over all the rest of America and Canada, even into Northern Mexico.

It must be remembered that the plan of the Danish Vikings who came to Askov was to raise pigs. But in order to do this, you need soil that would grow things for the pigs to eat. Growing things in rocks is difficult, and so the Vikings grew frustrated.

By contrast, the mindset of the Ojibwa was to accept the rocky ground cover and enjoy their days catching and eating the omega-3-laden bony and boneless fish that populated the Kettle River. They had learned to live with the natural order, and found the rocks great objects to sit on and look at. Just like the Yanomani along the Amazon, they lived with nature.

Let us not raise any embarrassing questions regarding IQs of these two cultures. We will merely observe that one chose to live enjoyably with nature while the other was hell bent on doing something about the existing rocky conditions.

It was at this first spring thaw that a sense of "we really got taken" by our forefathers began to set in. There was talk of returning to Denmark, but Vikings are proud people, and going back would be admitting they had been duped. Instead they began retelling dumb Molebo jokes they remembered from Jutland.

Like the earlier Danish visitors to Askov, it was during this stressful period that they, like their forefathers, discovered that you could take any kind of wild berry, ferment the bejeesus out of it, and get an acceptable libation. Drink lots of it quickly, and your mind would generate more new linguistic expressions, and laugh all the while doing it. And so it happened that the Danish language again exploded with new unintelligible guttural sounds.

Modern-day scholars, on grants, are still of uncertain and undocumented opinions that slugging a glass of ethanol, which is the genteel and socially accepted way to drink aquavit, initially began in the early Askovian era with the Ojibwa Native Americans. In Denmark you chase your slug of aquavit with a Tuborg, Carlsberg or Faxo.

Unlike the earlier Danish Vikings, these poor former pig farmers had no way of getting back to Denmark. During that first frigid winter they had burned their boats along with their worthless property deeds just to keep from freezing to death. Problem solving for survival now became a full time occupation.

This emerging calamitous situation created many ancillary problems. Some of the early religious, as well

as not-so-religious, souls began to think that only a for-
giving god, or a whole bunch of them, could get them
out of this mammoth rock pile that was covered with
snow and ice for at least nine months of the year. "Dis
vas an unholy mess."

Much of the dire religiosity generated at this time
came from depressed Swedes who had inadvertently
gotten caught up in the real estate sales pitches while
they were visiting Copenhagen to get drunk on weekends. It must have been quite an experience for these
homebody Swedes to be at one moment having the time
of their life in Copenhagen bistros and the next moment
trying to sober up in a rocking boat on the Atlantic
Ocean, wondering what had hit them . . . not to mention arriving months later, thoroughly confused, at the
frosty Askovian rock pile.

In Europe the Swedes and Danes do now sort of
coexist, but thank the gods that there is a body of cold
salt water between them. Recently they dug a tunnel
and built a bridge connecting the two nations, but only
the future can tell how successful this venture will be.

It is surmised that during this early immigration
period of grim adversity and frustration, many pioneer
religious sects were founded. It was not called foxhole
religion, but rather rock pile religion.

"Ve got to believe in something or ve vill go nuts,"
was their collective motto. All were wondering where
Thor and his cronies were now that they needed them.
Askov was for sure not the Viking Valhalla they had
heard so much about from their forefathers. To add to
their misery, the Askovian fish were discovered to be
bony pike, and none of them produced eatable caviar.

So they made up some new religions. Some of these
newly founded sects showed more interest in promot-

ing the entire silly Swedish concept of dread and guilt, while others were simply looking for an excuse to have a party. Since the days of yore, whenever that was, the Danes have been of the opinion that there is always room for one more religion, as long as it doesn't get in the way of a good party. So each of these little local splinter immigrant groupings began developing its own religious identity based on what they thought was in the mind of their creator. No doubt this is pretty much how all religions begin.

In adversity create your own creator to bail you out.

Start marketing the guy/gal—get converts.

Become rich, respected and powerful.

Prescription that — too often — works— too well.

On the issue of strict dogma, the Danish Vikings could not, for the sake of Thor and Odin, understand why the depressed Swedes were busily cooking up anti-drinking rules, when drinking was all that kept them from killing each other.

The less serious Danes survived. Some of them moved all over the Midwest, becoming known as the "Dancing Danes". Other more pious groups drifted into murkier places like Wisconsin, Nebraska, Iowa, and Missouri and became good gloomy conservative Lutherans. Tough times will do that to you.

This loosely concocted historical account is all that I really know about how the early Danes got settled in Askov. But get to Askov these Danish Vikings did, and it was "ja, for sure" not an easy trip and certainly a cold rocky surprise.

This fanciful account now gives way to more recent times, where events can be corroborated. Perhaps fantasy leads to reality.

Lesson Learned:

Do not take your history too seriously. You can't repeat it anyway.

Chapter 4
A Boundary Layer Begins

We now visit a specific immigrant, one of many who at the beginning of the twentieth century made the trip alone to America with only dreams and hopes— not an atypical immigrant for those times or for now.

Emil Andreas Hansen, born in 1888 in Listed, near Svanneke, on the little Danish island of Bornholm, in the Baltic Ocean, south of Sweden, left his home alone as a teenager. Before leaving he had worked on a windmill grinding grain. Whether or not he had been influenced by the earlier Danish Viking real estate scams he never divulged; he did have a lot of pride. An older brother and sister had made the exodus to America before him.

He came legally through New York's famous Ellis Island soon after the beginning of the twentieth century. In many ways he was probably just like many other alien teenagers who today cross American borders with a piece of paper, an empty stomach, and a desire to find a job.

Father did have legal immigration papers. But he came alone, had little money, no English language skills, and most importantly—no return ticket. This was it. He possessed most of the attributes mentioned in Chapter 1.

One can only assume he was excited, as well as profoundly scared. However, as we well know, male teenagers are by nature immortal, optimistic and able to take care of themselves in most situations, so my guess is he was exuberant, though hungry.

Father, or Far, as he was called in Danish, was very reluctant to ever divulge experiences from his childhood, and we never prodded. Like many poor immigrant kids, then and now, he did not have a particularly happy childhood to talk about. The finality and sadness of leaving his family and home on Bornholm Island at such an early age was an intense personal secret he could not bear to share, even with his own kids. We were certainly never burdened, or saddened, by any of his early unhappy experiences.

It is so tragic that many poor kids are often embarrassed kids. Why? They are certainly not responsible for their family's state of poverty. I have a hunch that impoverished immigrant's kids endure many harsh feelings that result from them wishing to somehow protect their parents. This is perhaps where boundary layer people begin learning how to make adjustments.

Only two childhood tales my father told stuck. One was about the time he had to have a tooth extracted. Dental work was primitive and expensive. First the dentist took a large pair of pliers and crushed his tooth, then piecemeal removed the fractured pieces. Naturally there was no Novocain or any other kind of painkiller, including aspirin. He said it bled and hurt a lot, but "you got over it."

The second story was about Christmas, when all the poor people were treated to a feast at the local church. He told how they would gorge themselves, then go out and up-chuck and return to do it again, because it tasted so good.

One can assume that with these kinds of early childhood experiences, getting a one-way trip to America looked promising. He never explained how he got the funds for a one-way trip, but I gather that his family of nine kids and two parents somehow chipped together. He was one of the younger siblings.

Many, if not most, immigrants from all nations who traveled to America at this time had poignant experiences to share. But because they felt no one would believe them, or they were simply ashamed of the experiences, they tended to bottle these memories up internally. As I was growing up in an immigrant community few of them ever talked about direct personal experiences in the old country; they had indeed cut the cord. While depressing, it may also be that these very hardships toughened them for adversity in their future.

A series of odd pickup jobs, some from other earlier immigrants and relatives, eventually led my father to Michigan and Illinois. He quickly learned English, though he never told us how. He had an excellent memory and was always focused. Relatives who attended his citizenship hearing related that he repeatedly bested the judge on many items of American history. He memorized facts, read vociferously, loved to write, and wanted to be a journalist, which was never to be. The judge complimented him on his knowledge of America. His goal in coming to America—citizenship—had been attained. He was ecstatic.

He got lucky, or so he thought, and was given a half-section (320 acres) of primordial unbroken sod in northeastern Montana on what had been Indian country. He acquired this property from American Indians under the famous, or infamous, Homestead Act of 1856. The land would be his permanently after living on it and tending it for many years. He was never very happy about this arrangement, nor, in all probability, were the displaced Native Americans who had thought they owned the desolate but beautiful plains.

The Homestead Act essentially took native lands from the American Indians and gave it to largely white, immigrant men, mostly European. This Montana land was harsh, barren, brutal and unplowed, ideally suited to its indigenous wildlife. Since it is a vast plain, the wind blew constantly; in the winter it was brutal. My father, who was single at the time, told me he was a most unhappy and lonesome homesteader. However he never regretted his decision to come to America.

Initially he owned a pair of huge oxen for "sod busting". Later, as relative prosperity set in, he was able to buy a steel wheeled behemoth of a tractor. This iron sodbuster had flat steel wheels with six-inch metal spikes for traction that would help chew up the soil ahead of the plow. These early sodbusters uncovered many Indian relics in the process of plowing, but my father refused to keep them. He felt strongly guilty about the manner in which he had become an American landowner at the expense of the Indians who had settled the land first.

Between oxen and tractors, my father and his distant neighbor immigrants tore the hell out of the virgin prairies of northeastern Montana. The activity of simply turning topsoil in order to grow wheat proceeded apace without much planning or thought for the future. This ludicrous farming practice helped contribute to a major disaster when the drought of the 1930s arrived. The dirt literally blew away.

When the First World War began, Father volunteered and was inducted into the army. But on the way to boot camp they discovered he had false teeth, a condition he had hidden during the induction process. I speculate that he saw the military as a patriotic duty, as well as a way of getting the hell off the farm, but now he was discharged and sent back to the farm. I do believe he sincerely missed going to the war in Europe, because he wanted to be a journalist. In later years he was an avid reader of history and war correspondents' reports; he loved their facts and details. Maps were always plentiful and studied.

There surely wasn't much to write about in northeastern Montana at this time, other than monotony, an endless blue sky, and a constantly blowing wind. Another depressing thought for him centered on the knowledge that his family in Bornholm had been mostly fishermen, plying the Baltic Sea and Atlantic Ocean like respectable seafaring Vikings. Here he was tethered to an isolated hunk of dusty former Indian land in the middle of nowhere. How humiliating. But he did not complain. He had made the decision to immigrate and had been successful in that decision. He was happy and proud of becoming an American.

In spite of disliking farming with a passion, it was providing a living, and in the early twenties a very good living. He traveled to Denmark in style, not in steerage as he had on the first trip. He always said that it just cost a little bit more to go first class. At the time he could afford it, being single and relatively well off.

If these Danish immigrants suffered from depression due to their circumstances, they surely did not let on. Instead they seemed to develop a sense of absurd humor to get them through the tough spots. Luckily some of that rubbed off on the boundary layer folks.

The next thing that happened to my father was my mother-to-be, Gudrun Marianne Paulsen, a young Danish lady who had grown up as a child in the Askovian Rock Capitol, and who now came to teach country normal school in this rock-less, dusty area of Montana. Here she met her husband and my father-to-be, and there you have it.

I was born in a town called Plentywood, Montana, close to midnight—so close they couldn't agree on the date, but settled on July 2, 1929. This was another sign of sick humor—in Plentywood there wasn't a tree as far as the eye could see, and that was half way to the planet Pluto. Plentywood was probably an Indian name that got screwed up in translation. At my birth the coyotes howled and the wind blew, because that is what happens every night in Plentywood. I was given the name Viggo, probably Viking in origin—at least I hope so.

Plentywood boasted, according to the prominent Fort Peck Publication of the 1920's, that it was

"Prosperous, Progressive,
   The place with the Punch.
Plenty rain, plenty grain,
plenty stock and plenty money.
   Plentywood sets the pace."   Oh boy!

Only the gods that be would know what they were drinking when they concocted this ad for their Sheridan

County Seat newspaper.

The three of us left Plentywood for a smaller town called Richland, consisting of a grain elevator, a general store, and a very dusty street. This was the village that was closest to my father's property. There was also Scobey nearby, whose name denotes a special kind of geology. Further south you have Glasgow, the county seat. Then there was Fort Peck, of historical fame, and whose name was later attached to the then world's largest earth-built dam.

Richland environs are flat with gently rolling hills; you get the impression you can see forever, and as a kid you can. The view is captivating; the landscape is a panoply of light and dark variegated green native grasses interspersed with fields of golden grains, mostly wheat. This had been the Garden of Eden for all those buffaloes that had a few short years before ranged freely and provided the Indians with a natural lifestyle.

Experiencing the wind blowing across a field of wheat seemingly gives one a perspective into the infinite. It is like watching the winds moving across an open body of water. There literally are waves of bending wheat stalks, stretching from horizon to horizon across the moderately hilly land, rising and falling like golden ocean swells. Not only is the sight of waving grain beards spellbinding, but you also hear a swishing sound as the beards brush against each other. It is as though they are talking and singing among themselves, a sound as distinctive as the ocean waves.

Every time I hear the song "Blowin' in the Wind," popular in the sixties and seventies, I experience a wave of nostalgia for those early years of listening to the wind in the wheat. I suspect one could make the case that the landlocked Danish immigrants adjusted to enjoying the sea of bending and flowing wheat almost as much as the rollicking Baltic Ocean, with no mal de mer.

Now, many years later, having taken up doing a little sailing, I can see these earlier experiences with waving wheat fields prepared me to feel at ease with waves of saltwater waves and the accompanying ocean swells.

These early sounds of the prairie in my childhood were certainly different from the sounds of a large city like Los Angeles, which later became my home. The prairie sounds are deep and long; they convey a sense of infinite extension. The prairie listener has a feeling of being in tune with the cosmos, especially at night when the stars add their twinkling, but nonetheless steadying, influence.

On the prairie at night, when stars twinkle at you and the wind blows softly across fields of grain, you feel a deep personal unity with nature—a sense of forever. It is profoundly otherworldly . . . eerie.

Having lived on the barren open prairie and in compacted cities, I find it interesting to contrast the two environments in a variety of ways.

While the sounds of the prairie are quieting and soothing, the sounds of the city are urgent and penetrating. They scream for immediate attention and action, all the while cutting deeply into one's inner self. At night the garish neon lights shine insistently rather than twinkle. One's perspective and interpretation of city lights and sounds are certainly not in concert with the prairie's outer universe perspective.

Perhaps the city is what it is like to be inside an atom, and the prairie is more like open space—a microcosmos versus a mega-cosmos. Hopefully physicists with their super string theories will some day find an explanation that unifies these divergent perspectives.

I am not certain that my father's early starry nights on the plains, when he was alone in his low-ceilinged house with no phone or close neighbors and coyotes howling all about were all that romantic. I am sure he was probably scared, generally hungry, and finding it difficult to earn a living.

Perhaps even more troubling was the uncertainty of how well the Indians were taking to the Homestead Act. Again I am reminded how lucky first generations are in reaping the benefits of the immigrants' strength, courage, and humility. It should make first generations a humble bunch, but I am not sure we have always acted that way.

My life on the prairie as a tot was very lonesome, but in that isolation one gets well acquainted with oneself, since that is all you got. Like any child growing up in loneliness, you are forced to be creative or go mad. Our farm was in the boonies, miles from Richland's dusty street—yes, there was just one. We had no close neighbors, and only on the rare occasions when we made a major journey for our meager provisions to Scobey or Richland, did I see other people. There was also a Danish Lutheran church somewhere that we visited on special occasions. We made these dusty journeys in a Model T Ford over trails that wound around fields and gullies.

Finding arrowheads was a thrill-filled and suspenseful activity on the prairie. Mother, as all mothers do, took advantage of this mundane activity to create an adventure. Her constant stream of questions and "keep looking" admonitions did indeed make these moments precious. As mentioned earlier we did find Indian relics, which mother carefully collected, against my father's wishes because of his feelings about the deposed Indians. As the years went by this modest collection disappeared, and I guess it's just as well.

I was lucky to begin my childhood with turkeys as playmates. Turkeys, who must date back to prehistoric times, are mean and unforgiving bastards, but they do teach you to be wary and tough. Their pointed beaks at the end of a strong, fast-moving neck provide them with a platform of authority that few dare challenge. I vaguely remember crawling up haystacks and jumping off, trying to emulate their primitive flying skills. Turkeys, though classified as birds, have a ratio of weight to wing area that does not support flight, but chased off of a haystack they sort of glide like a thrown flat rock, all the while cackling like banshees in heat.

On one of my haystack jumps while merrily chasing mad turkeys, I landed improperly, i.e., on my head, and stayed knocked out for a few days. When I got old enough my parents told me they had almost given up on my making it. Perhaps the turkeys had toughened me physically for the ordeal; mentally, however, I was never the same!

Lightning storms on the prairie, a rather frequent summertime event, provided a level of fear, terror, and excitement that as a child you never forgot. I remember once when a gazillion-volts lightning bolt struck our small tool shed and zapped through a large iron crowbar, making it glowing red.

Often the thunderclaps came almost concurrently with the flash of lightning, giving you no time to prepare for the subsequent deafening sound waves; this really scared out your vital juices. Sometimes I would defiantly scream back at the thunder, as in tit for tat. Challenging nature's fury is something everyone likes to do at one time or another. This was it for me.

Mother was a fantastic storyteller, as was her mother, as was her mother. These prairie storms were the perfect setting for her to teach about our mythical Nordic forefathers, Odin, Thor, Gideon, Loki, the Valkyries, et al. I still remember her attempts to sooth my jangled nerves during those hellish electrical storms by telling me to visualize the great god Thor riding across the skies, throwing out lightning bolts and making enough noise to wake the dead. I surmised that because Thor had somewhere important to go in a hurry, it was necessary for him to scare us kids out of our wits.

Later on in life one recalls these thunder and light shows with Viking pride, as they become the source of much laughter and excuses for drinking homemade wine and aquavit. Perhaps these intense nocturnal prairie experiences with pagan gods, laced with homespun prairie Lutheranism, produced a cautious attitude towards any established religion being sacrosanct.

An aside: it is in retrospect that I remember my Uncle Joe, whom you will meet in more detail in a later chapter, talking with me about the problems humankind has had in always creating gods that are too small and anthropomorphic. By god, a good booming Montana prairie fire-and-brimstone thunderstorm in the dead of night will for sure expand one's concept of the providential, especially when a child.

For those folks who have always worshipped gods too small, they should spend some quality time on the prairie in a goddamn thunderstorm. Then, as the skies begin clearing and twinkling stars reappear in a seemingly infinite universe, you do put manmade gods into perspective.

Some years ago I was fortunate to have a private

dinner with scientist Dr. Buckminister Fuller, the creative engineering genius of our century. Geodesic domes and dymaxion cars.

I asked him, "Dr. Fuller, how did you come to create geodesic domes?"

He replied that I was the first one to ask him that question, but that he had pondered this and felt it was because he was very nearsighted as a child and could only focus to fifty feet or so in any direction.

"Thus, I was living in a dome of a radius of fifty feet. Later, when my family could afford eyeglasses, I was shocked to see how big this world really is."

True story.

Perhaps the isolated prairie farmers, the lonely sailors at sea, and the astronomers are the folks in closest touch with the real magnitude of the universe. As our observatories, on land and in the sky, take us further back in time, they are in effect experiencing a limited view of the universe, as was the case with Buckminster Fuller's eyesight.

Until our "vision" is clear, we can only infer what lies beyond. And that is tricky business.

We all live in bubbles, and we can easily make the case that our bubbles are always too small, both physically and intellectually.

The bigger that bubble, the bigger your universe becomes.

The early years spent on Montana's prairie did produce deep memories that still linger. In trying to analyze why this is so, I am convinced that since we had few distractions, like siblings, radio, television, play-mates, and so on, we had to devise a mental world out of our own thoughts. Daydreaming and watching cumulus clouds drift quietly by was acceptable behavior for a kid in this time and place.

Reverie is still a great activity when you don't wish to interact with all the noise that surrounds us in our everyday world. It is fun to watch the Japanese commuters in Tokyo subways as their heads bob endlessly back and forth while they hurtle through manmade rat tubes. You gotta hope they are into some kind of inner space.

Again, it is this lucky first generation that early in their lives learned from their immigrant parents to seek comfort and strength from within. Boundary layer kids are forced to solve their own problems as best they can.

Lesson Learned:

Prairie beginnings are great

Because -
You learn to live in a big bubble.

The Richland, Montana homestead circa 1930.

Chapter 5
Depression—
Movin' On

The infamous American Great Depression, which officially began in 1929, the year of stock market collapse and my birth, was by the early thirties settling in with vengeance throughout the world. Republican President Herbert Hoover had stated in 1928, "We in America today are nearer to the final triumph over poverty than ever before in the history of any land."

But by 1932 that bellicose statement had a superbly hollow sound as factories ground almost to a standstill and production dropped to at best fifty percent of just a few years earlier. The creative assembly lines that had produced so many inexpensive products for Americans were now in financial trouble.

Money problems were brutal for both the poor working factory immigrants and the immigrant farmers in their fields. Twenty-five percent unemployment was the norm in the cities. Few crops were the norm for the farmer. The American dream was becoming a nightmare. A sense of hopelessness was leading to labor unrest in the cities and despair among the poverty-stricken farmers who were unable to grow and sell their crops.

The smart-ass conservative businessmen of the time had come face to face with the results of the run-amuck capitalism of that period. However, some of these misguided conservative concepts had been the outgrowth of the immigrants' own individualistic traditions as they moved across the land and established new industries based on almost limitless resources and few restrictions.

Could this have been the beginning of America's self-indulgence?

Clearly changes had to be made, and in 1932 Franklin D. Roosevelt became America's leader to make these changes. His wealthy background did not seem to blur his vision of helping the poor and downtrodden. He was a polished "can do" type American, and he got to work immediately.

For farmers, the overall depressed state of affairs were the result of a combination of factors: extremely low income from their meager crops due to lack of moisture, and very conservative monetary policies enacted by the controlling Republican Congress. Politics were now being paid attention to, by both the farmers and the laborers. Could the American government and its politics solve the problem? Luckily this "can do" rescue program was formulated to save the nation.

Roosevelt's "New Deal" was about to begin changing America forever. The plan was a very bold move for a relatively young nation. But with a broad-based appealing concept and Roosevelt's elocution skills, the

New Deal took root. Though somewhat slow in coming, a wide spectrum of Americans began experiencing enthusiasm. The good times were coming back—slowly. Politically things were not going at all well in Europe. Many American immigrants, especially European, now viewed Hitler as a madman and a potentially big problem, but to a large extent this German threat was overshadowed by the economic problems on America's home front. Isolationism had a large numbers of supporters. However the Danish immigrants in America, who were always, and still are, suspicious of what the Germans might be up to, were beginning to express serious concerns. World War I was still a grim memory across much of Europe.

The farming practices used by the immigrant sodbusters in northeastern Montana were finally recognized as having been misguided and disastrous. But concepts of protecting the virgin topsoil by terracing, rotating fields, and using a variety of crops had not yet been developed. As a result these grain farmers were rapidly being starved out—no rain, no crops, no food. The "dust bowl" extended from Oklahoma to Canada with no relief in sight.

At night the winds, saturated with invisible dust particles, howled and screamed through our modest home, making it difficult to sleep. By day the sky was sickly yellow with this dust that made for constant coughing and choking.

Frequently huge black ominous clouds of grasshoppers would pass through and eat the few remaining stalks of grain that had found enough water to sprout. Some of these varmints were six inches long and really frightening to see as they moved; hopping, crawling, flying, and always screaming across our yard and surrounding fields.

The hapless farmers, hoping to find a clue to stopping the deadly onslaught, earnestly studied passages from the Old Testament regarding locusts. Praying was about the only weapon these desperate farmers were able to learn from their biblical investigations, however. The drought persisted, and the grasshoppers continued their feeding frenzy.

It was definitely time to recognize the futility of farming without adequate moisture and to accept the inevitable conclusion to cease farming on the homesteaded Indian land in Montana. Farmers would gather in small groups, since there weren't many of them to begin with, and lament their predicament.

I clearly remember my folks at night, in tears, reluctantly admitting to themselves that what they had toiled sohard for had to be let go. They had lost just about everything, and "Ja, for sure," no one wanted to buy their useless land, which by now had become legally theirs. Since there were no buyers, they had to keep it or give it back to the state. Taxes were extremely low, so they kept it. What they didn't know till much later was that the Williston oilfield lay several thousand feet right below them.

Keep in mind there were few social services or support systems to fall back on when the immigrant fell on hard luck. For my immigrant father, the situation felt like his earlier days when he had left Bornholm with only hope; but now he also had bigger responsibilities—a family.

After agonizing over their condition, my parents finally decided it was time for us to leave the hard-earned homestead. Time and money had run out.

"But to go where and to do what?" my parents constantly asked. Like for other unproductive and unemployed immigrants of this period, there were few promising or enticing answers.

In other parts of America, many destitute people were drifting westward. "Go west, young man" was again reverberating across the land. I know California and Oregon were under consideration as my parents pondered our future.

Wouldn't you know it—they decided to load up their remaining meager possessions and haul off to Askov! Ja, sure. You remember Askov, where in earlier times roustabout Vikings had fished sturgeons and cavorted on the rocky banks of the Kettle River? We were not going west, we were going east!

Recall that it was eons earlier that the first wave of Danish Vikings had gotten frozen out of Askov and returned to Denmark to sell snow-covered property to the restless and adventuresome folks at home. The second group of numbskulls, those who bought the bogus deeds, had by now, through hard labor and diligence, established roots in the area. Askov was also the town where my mother had come from before going to Montana. Segments of her family, including my grandmother still lived there. So...

Hi ho, it was off to Askov we would go, in a beatup Model T Ford with a bad timer. This device, used to keep sparkplugs firing at the proper time, is one of humankind's most fascinating inventions, the essential part of motor engines of that period.

This high adventure was to take us from the rolling plains, grasshoppers, and dust storms of arid Montana to the mosquito-infested uncontested rock capitol of the world. Details of this trek, which it surely was, fade in and out of my memory. As I recall, our initial travel manifest included two parents, my sister, several cats and a dog, and me.

The animals got terribly car sick, along with the rest of us, so we periodically stopped at farms in the godforsaken barren state of North Dakota to see if some softhearted farmer might not need a loving pet. Luckily for our furry traveling companions, we did find compassionate families who willingly assumed responsibility for these unhappy travelers. That is why I still love North Dakota—it is populated by some really wonderful people and just maybe also by descendants of our cats and dog.

As we slowly puttered along dusty trails and finally entered the western edges of Minnesota, I saw for the first time large green plants, which the natives called trees. They looked to me incredibly beautiful and yet awesome. Five years of life on the plain had not prepared me for this experience. Suddenly the birthplace name Plentywood lost it's meaning, or took on a new one.

My frame of reference was happily shifting from a dry, barren ecosystem to one that was lush and humid. There were some downsides, however. One in particular was a small flying prehistoric bloodsucking insect that with lightning speed stuck you at a spot that later itched enough to drive you mad. This was, is, and will remain the infamous Minnesota mosquito, often referred to as their state bird.

The endless array of lakes and rivers that we seemed to drive along were absolutely spellbinding. Getting our feet and hands into this wet stuff was a real treat. We would frequently stop and just romp along the water's edge, much as the Vikings of old had described in their sagas about the Askovian Kettle River.

There were croaking frogs and dragonflies, and occasionally a fish would break the water's surface—all very new and delightful experiences.

The facts that the old man did not have a job, had very little money, owned only a dilapidated Model T that was constantly breaking down, all our pets were now scattered somewhere across North Dakota, and so on, did not seem to be important at those moments. Here was all that blue water surrounded by fresh green stuff. Western Minnesota was most beautiful.

But we unfortunately did not stop. Oh, no, we just kept puttering eastward leave a tiny dusty trail.

After awhile we began seeing big hard things along the dusty roadside; these were called rocks. They came in a wide assortment of irregular shapes. Some were small enough to pick up and toss, while others were big enough to sit on. Slowly a geological transition was taking place right before our very eyes: fewer lakes and more rocks. It was an omen of things to come.

For just a moment let us fast-forward about fifty years. In looking back at this "Great Depression" period, I believe we, the nomad farmer families, looking for a place to live, were indeed the lucky ones in that we were able to move. Something about having the ability to move is somehow reassuring. As one's mobility becomes more restricted with age, a sense of claustrophobic panic begins to seep in as one begins anticipating a completely immobile future.

When Father later became incapacitated due to a stroke, the most depressing and frightening thing for him was that he knew he would no longer be able to drive a car. Indeed he became confined to a wheel chair without the ability to talk or feed himself. For the adventuresome immigrants who gave so much of themselves to obtain freedom, the inability to move was the ultimate disaster.

Looking at today's media pictures of people throughout the world running from one calamity after another, I am convinced that the attitude and capacity to simply move is highly reassuring and is what gives people hope in their most desperate moments. The desire, as well as ability, to change locations defines the immigrants, who tend to be restless.

My parents often told us how lucky we were to be able to travel around the countryside looking for a new home and new jobs to do. The poor city folks were not so fortunate; they had never lived on the prairie in northeastern Montana! In truth, unemployed immigrant city folks during the Great Depression era were stuck in their urban caverns. This had to be most difficult, like being in prison. The strikes, food lines, and homelessness that existed in the thirties were surely as bad or worse than the conditions that beset the deposed farmers. This was a very tough period in America's history. Had it not been for the indomitable spirit of the immigrants, on the farms and in the cities, the nation might not have survived.

This historical time period, defined by the financial depression and unemployment, was the last time large farm migrations took place within America. As the policies of the New Deal and World War II kicked in, the farmers gradually became more settled, and many became prosperous.

This state of affairs of individually owned farms was to change radically after the Second World War, when large corporations began gobbling up the small, single-family farms. This time the out-of-farming farmer had no place to go but into other kinds of employment, which usually meant moving into the cities.

Today's successful farms are in every sense businesses, indeed corporations in many cases. The intimacy of raising crops and animals has shifted. Modern scientific techniques provide for robotic, controlled equipment that is directed by global positioning satellites. These innovations are stripping away the human farming experience of being close to nature.

A disturbing result of this transition is that, when we are individually no longer close to nature, we are less responsive to nature's frailties and begin to take its bounties for granted. A bad move, as the prairie sodbusters found out in the thirties.

Leaving the Richland grain growing community under the prevailing circumstances was of course sad, but on the other hand I remember that once the decision was made, my family felt a certain enthusiasm. My parents stopped lamenting their loss and began anticipating the future. Another new adventure had begun. This immigrant characteristic of being able to let go is another of the benefits that are bestowed on the "boundary layer people." You learn to accept your losses and move forward with hope.

The financial depression and untenable climatic conditions that prevailed in Montana led to the acceptance of a truism, that goes something like: If you know you can't beat 'em, then by golly it is best to pack up your motley stuff and quietly move on.

In summary, the prairie life provided me a profound beginning, including fantastic endless vistas, spectacular sound and light shows at night, and a half section of erstwhile Indian Land nobody now wanted to buy.

Lessons Learned:

When it is time to move—it is time to move.

Yes—it became another migration adventure

Chapter 6
Arrival

The dust-caked rickety Model T Ford was gasping and sputtering fitfully as we drove over the single-lane creaking wooden bridge spanning the mighty Kettle River. The crossing of the awesome Kettle River marked our official entry into Askov. It had been an exciting journey of many eventful days.

The earlier grief at leaving "home" was replaced by the joy of arriving and beginning a new home.

Moving is not all bad — a lesson learned from America's immigrants.

Like the earliest Danish Vikings, we arrived dirty and weary, but there were no Ojibwa chiefs or members of their tribe to meet us. The only place we could find to live was an abandoned farmhouse several miles north of Askov. The good news was we had a grandmother in town who was most loving and supportive, and always had warm milk and cookies. Over the years she was to teach us kids to write and improve our speaking ability in our native language of Danish. She and my grandfather, who had died some years before, had been pioneers in Askov—though we never discussed property deeds.

The first thing you must to learn when moving into the Greater Metropolitan Askovian Community is that there is a strictly adhered to Social Register. This Registry is reported to have been started by Sven, Olaf, and their wives many years earlier to maintain order and preserve the history of the immigrants. The names that end in -sen are in the elite category. Those ending with -son are probably descendents from some luckless Swedes and Norse who drunkenly strayed into the early Danish Viking boats, thus are considered a cut below. Names like Sandahl, Krantz, Sebald, Stovring and the like make up a mystery group found scattered throughout the registry.

As a bitter winter set in, it was butt cold in our mouse- and other varmint-infested farmhouse. Cow dung, mud, and whatever, was used as caulking material in an attempt to keep the cold out and heat in. Freshly cut wood from poplar and pine trees with an occasional piece of coal served as heating and cooking fuel. Kerosene provided fuel for lights. Windows were mostly covered over, since glass is an excellent conductor of cold. This visually restricted any view of our new surroundings, making it fun to be outside just to see where we were.

We eventually acquired a couple of cows, two horses, and some chickens to launch our basic farming unit. Father, who in general hated farming anyhow, was even less thrilled at having to go from being a grain farmer to being a dairy farmer, with all the constraints this incurred. In Askov you did not simply plant seeds, like wheat, and then wait to harvest it. Now, cows demanded twice daily attention for milking, feeding, and cleaning, 24—7.

Periodically the human body needs to remove materials it no longer deems essential for survival. To accommodate this condition Askovians had designed what was euphemistically called an "outhouse"—a small rectangular wooden structure housing two large circles cut in a bench. This edifice was situated above a deep hole in the ground, far away from the house. Often the door had a carving of a half moon. The origin of this primitive art form is unknown.

In this interesting and useful structure, where temperatures ranged from a degree above absolute zero to a degree below the sun's surface, you quickly learned split-second control over two major bodily functions. These early-acquired biological control skills were essential to keep Askovians from freezing or boiling to death at crucial times. Later in life these early acquired physiological "controls" became especially valuable in the military - ja, sure.

Somehow until the spring of 1935, now at the age of six, I had eluded the formality of attending public school, since we never lived near one. But it was March, roads were now regularly open, and it was decided that it was time I should begin getting an education at the H. C. Andersen schoolhouse in Askov. Home schooling was no longer an option.

Hans Christian Andersen, the noted Danish storyteller—author of serious tales like, "The Emperor's New Clothes," "The Ugly Duckling," "The Little Match Girl," and the like—had a strong influence on many Danish immigrants and their offspring. Askovians assumed that since he had been an outstanding author and educator, it would be appropriate to name their school after him. Good thought.

Andersen's stories, through many translations, have now been enjoyed throughout the world. He addresses adult themes, but with childlike innocence and in mythical settings, as in "The Little Mermaid." One comes away from reading Hans's tales with a message that is both captivating and thought provoking, but seldom flippant. These fairy tales engage the reader in significant issues, like the story of the poor little match girl freezing to death, gazing in the windows of a rich storekeeper. Today the store would be called "Life at Enron." Stories like these have probably contributed immeasurably to the evolving social welfare society representative of today's Denmark.

Andersen's narratives are not in the same genre as most other tales or books supposedly written for children. You don't have to do much serious thinking when you are in Oz, for example, but you do when you read about the "Emperor's New Clothes." His stories came with an adult message. His theory, aside for enjoying story telling, was perhaps that if as a child you learned compassion through a fantasy it would later translate into adult behavior.

Contrasting these rather innocent stories with some of today's computer controlled video gaming makes for interesting discussions. Andersen's tales were and are thought provoking—today's violent video games are pure visceral reactions.

At the H. C. Andersen schoolhouse, located at the corner of town with its prominent bell tower, they spoke what seemed to me a funny language called English. Being a native speaker of medieval Danish, I found this new language a challenge. The approach we were given is called, in today's educational parlance, "immersion in a second language," i.e., sink or swim. For sure this was initially a confusing experience, but still it is a far superior approach than today's bilingual approach, where often the frustrated kids end up, after a long confusing period of time, knowing neither language.

Language acquisition is always a major issue for non-English-speaking immigrants. Today the problem is much broader, with the plethora of different languages compounded by the fact that some immigrants now seemingly do not wish to become English literate. But again it is the "boundary layer people" who benefit most from being forced to acquire at least two languages, rather than the one of their parents.

Over the years of being in the education business, I have concluded that perhaps the very best approach to learning the English language (or any foreign language) is to first learn some swear/cuss words. Use them frequently and loudly. You immediately gain peer recognition, most important for kids. From there on you can easily learn the other stuff, and all the while nobody pokes fun at you.

As a child I quickly picked up a few English cuss words and started using them liberally. As a result of learning vulgarity, I was immediately accepted by my peers. Indeed, they were eager to teach me more naughty words, so I also became popular, except with parents and other adults. (Just an aside: learning these "bad" words really had no special significance for me. The words did not carry any emotional component whatsoever. They were simply sounds that attracted attention, much as a child's crying captures the attention of its mother.)

It is strange, but to this very day certain words mean more to me in Danish than the same concepts expressed in English. They are words like love, hate, mother, father, God, etc. These are the words that, when first learning to communicate as a child, you realize are very important, and you don't forget the feelings associated with them, be they good or bad.

First-language words are emotionally charged - subsequent languages less so.

As America continues to struggle with incorporating non-native English speakers, I believe we are witnessing a lessening in the "naughtiness " of words. The acceptance of vulgarity is most pronounced in the tedious and obnoxious verbal expressions used by many of today's self-proclaimed comedians, who somehow think it is cute and chic to ramble on endlessly with these empty, but perceived naughty expressions. The positive side is that the more these twits use them, the sooner they become boring and fade away.

Perhaps this constant overuse of vulgarities is simply a reflection that their users no longer view these expressions in any serious way; the words carry little emotional load, serving merely as attention getters.

As new words are tried out on parents and other adults, we quickly learn which words are acceptable in one situation but are upsetting in another. This is when a sense of the power of language skills really becomes evident. In today's world, society at large and educators are still sadly and ineffectively debating which esoteric language-training program is most effective. A suggestion: Let the kids first learn Cussing 101, and then move on.

The second early school lesson I learned in becoming an English speaker was that peers are the real teachers. Kids know what is what and are most eager to share this knowledge with others.

Often we forget that the real teachers in schools are the kids.

Since Hans Christian Andersen had been a renowned storyteller, we decided that out of respect to good old HCA, the telling of stories to cover our problems was probably within the bounds of the school's mission statement. We started polishing the fine art of lying. In today's parlance we challenged each other with, "What kind of spin would HC put on this situation?" Telling stories was considered acceptable, even admirable. And so it is with kids everywhere.

There is an interesting aside here, and that is how adults, mainly parents, entertain their kids by making up stories, some of them completely outlandish.

I have often wondered, at what level in human development do kids realize that the stuff being told to them by well meaning adults is mostly nonsense? I find it fascinating to observe how children mature. Jule Nisse and Santa Claus magically become warm fuzzy childhood memories that we continue to adore, regardless of how old and cynical we become.

How quietly, but quickly, innocence gives way to a harsh reality.

Our school was a joyful place, with good friends and teachers. We got a small peanut butter sandwich and sometimes a piece of fruit for lunch. Above all, our school had indoor plumbing and was warm in winter. Life was indeed getting better, and I began to entertain thoughts of becoming a teacher. The goal of working in such a grand building as opposed to shoveling stinking manure in a dark cold barn began to make a lot of sense.

Contrasts are valuable motivating assets when making decisions.

A good guess is that an overwhelming number of immigrant parents encouraged their kids to go into education. "Get as close to the smarts are as you can." Instinctively these immigrants knew that the road to success was paved with books and guided by teachers. Anecdotal evidence seems to suggest that American classrooms at all levels, kindergarten through graduate school, have an inordinately large percentage of immigrants' children in the teaching business.

In elementary school we did lots of naughty things, but they were never elevated into a federal case as now happens all too often. There were parameters to acceptable behavior that everyone understood as being sacrosanct, but within them we had lots of opportunities to be bad. Growing up was seen as a time to be experimental and to have some fun.

Another characteristic of education in H.C. Andersen was the lack of emphasis on grades. When you came home from school, the questions were about "how did you get along?" and "tell us" what you learned today. Seldom were we asked, "What grade did you get?" Our marks were of little concern compared with behavior and adjustment to teachers and colleagues.

Childhood was the supreme time for personal activity-oriented research. During this period of restricted freedom, each child had an opportunity and an obligation to decide for themselves just what in hell life is all about. We could test the limits, but we were never allowed to exceed them. Unfortunately for many kids today, school has become over-stimulating, regimented, terrifying, and stressful. We were the lucky generation when it came to basic education, which was defined much more broadly than a number on a transcript. Present-day schools face security issues completely unthinkable in the 1930s and 40s. No one could conceive of going into a school with weapons intended to harm others, let alone blowing themselves up at the end of the process. It is interesting to note that the violent behavior witnessed in today's schools is seldom, if ever, done by an immigrant kid.

We experienced some pressure to pass exams, but never in our wildest dreams would the Askovian community, in those days, have adopted today's "high stakes" testing malarkey. The Askovian immigrants had learned long before that society needs a wide range of abilities and skills. Cookie cutter approaches *don't* cut it when it comes to educating people to be creative and self-fulfilling.

We are now destroying many of the happiest moments of American children due to the way our schools conduct their educational evaluations. The efforts of our society to increase productivity by hammering school children to improve their test scores is totally ridiculous, and may even be counterproductive, leading to poorer performance and grosser aberrant behavior.

Many years after my days at Andersen School, while giving a PTA talk on the topic of the misguided "new math", I was looking at a science essay written by a fourth grader. The teacher had peppered the article with big red ovals between each word. She had offered not a single comment on the content of the student's work. I asked the teacher about all those red ovals. She took my right hand, took two fingers next to the thumb, and put them on the red ovals, proudly saying that the student hadn't left two fingers of space between the words.

Gee whiz. Maybe the little nipper simply had small fingers.

With this inane emphasis on arbitrary and artificial standards, and less concern for the content, it is no wonder that so many students become frustrated and confused by what they should be doing. Where in the world did this teacher learn the "two finger" writing rule? It renders the entire process of teacher training and staff development a ridiculous sphincter tightening exercise if these are the kinds of standards that must be met.

As for the language acquisition business, which every immigrant's kid has to conquer, for me, the process was often both challenging and downright fun. First generation kids had to learn to mix words and sounds, to create acceptable behavior patterns from two cultures, sand to ensure that whatever we said or did was not complete gibberish or insulting. It is these kinds of amalgamating experiences that give rise to the rich Americana we all enjoy. Good ole Askovian H. C. Andersen School should receive high marks for accomplishing these tasks over the many years it faithfully served the immigrants.

It is absolutely essential that early childhood education and/or schooling be the quintessential experience in any kid's life. The process of discovering how to use our brain in a compassionate, honest, yet playful manner is the greatest challenge facing all societies. Schools set the tone and standards for the rest of each person's life.

America still has a lot of tough sledding to do to make education a meaningful reality for all students in all our schools. Schools designed by some of our immigrants, e.g., normal school for training teachers, should perhaps be given a second look.

The move from the prairie was now complete. Mooing, demanding dairy cows had replaced the endless fields of softly waving wheat. School had become the focus for the present, while the sharing social attitudes exemplified by Danish immigrants were taking hold. Life was again good.

Lesson Learned:

Do not be afraid of new beginnings.

Read and believe in good fairy tales.

A whimsical version of a Nordic Sailing craft.

Chapter 7
Death Makes a Call

We often observe that with any risk come additional risks, almost as if they compound as time goes along. Immigrants to America accepted the risk that in coming here, they might incur a higher probability of an early death than if they stayed home. They developed a unique attitude toward mortality.

In elementary school one picks friends fearlessly based on some kind of intuition or chemistry. These early friendships cannot be forced. And so it was that Arne became one of my best friends in the second grade. Arne was a city boy, but he loved to be on the farm, because there were so many options for things to do— one of which was playing in the manure pile. We weren't looking for any stray ponies, either.

As second graders we had become close friends to the point where we tried to be together whenever possible, be it at school or in our homes on weekends. Our activities were the simple things, like playing with self-made toys and digging holes wherever possible. We shared a wagon that served many purposes. We sure as hell never talked about death.

It is uncertain just when the concept of death becomes meaningful to a kid. Like most children, we attended funerals for older people that we did not know well. If the deceased was a family member or a close relative, the occasion was certainly more intense, but the ceremonies usually ended with good food and constantly being told to be quiet. Along with the hugging and crying, the adults often told humorous stories about the departed to ease the loss.

But when does death move beyond the stage of unreality to the realization that this is a very special, one-of-a-kind event? I sense that today our media and real world events have so desensitized kids to death that it is too often a non-event for them, even into adulthood. Everybody does seemingly die, but somehow they really don't. Perhaps this is an emerging awakening to a new age—a subject I'll address later.

For me, death became very real one fateful spring Saturday when my city friend Arne came to spend the day on our farm. The morning passed quickly in play and eating mother's cookies. After lunch Arne went across the road to the Fredricksens', who had a very large and efficient farm that was amply populated with kids both older and younger than Arne and me. In their backyard they had a beautiful flower-decked rock garden. Here the word *rock* is redundant, since all of Askov is rock; *garden* is to soothe that condition.

Over this sunken, sweet-smelling garden grew a large tree with branches just begging to be climbed by seven-year-old boys. Up the tree scampered Arne; near the end of a long branch he slipped and fell headfirst onto a rock. He never regained consciousness. During the afternoon I would occasionally go in and look at my sleeping friend as his now greatly shortened life ebbed slowly and silently away. With no doctors or ambulances readily available in those days, Arne slept in the Fredricksen house until his time to die arrived later in the afternoon.

When word reached my folks, they told me Arne had fallen out of the tree and would no longer be able to play with me. At first I did not really understand what this was all about, but I felt a strange numbness and a frigid, icy feeling running through my body.

That evening Arne's and my father sat quietly in our modest living/dining room talking about the tragedy that had just befallen us all. I remember sobbing very quietly in a corner trying to sort out the enormity of the situation, which I was just beginning to grasp. I had seen many animals die, indeed assisted in killing some, but had until now never been close to a human my age who had just "crossed the bar". A certain childish optimism assured me that Arne and I would soon again be playing together, the sense of finality still remaining elusive.

Arne had been the only male child in his family, and in those days this somehow was viewed as a greater loss than if it had been one of his sisters. It wasn't stated just that way, more like "he was our only son". I remember picking up on that comment from his father and not really knowing what was meant. I, too, was an only son. This attitude, mostly unspoken, is of course still prevalent in many parts of the world today.

Vividly I remember how our second grade class quietly collected the tiny blue spring violets that grew abundantly along moist roadsides and in the small creeks near our school. After picking them we went inside to weave a flower chain that would be placed on Arne's simple homemade wooden casket.

The loss of our childhood friend was poorly understood and did not pass easily. Sadness and emptiness hung depressingly heavy in our little classroom for many weeks. The teacher led discussions on the fun times we had experienced with Arne, and how now it was time for the rest of us to move on. Thus it was that at age seven, death became a frightening and meaningful concept to me. Life does flow relentlessly onward, seemingly in only one direction, and we are all carried by that flow called time. But for a moment that flow had stopped. Death was damn real.

For many weeks following the loss of Arne, I would find myself talking to him while playing, as though he was still there. Who knows, maybe he was.

Whenever there was a death in Askov, and there were many, the immigrants quietly demonstrated a level of communal strength and acceptance that carried us all forward. This stoic Danish immigrant attitude was probably the result of their having sacrificed much in order to get to this new world. The attitude might translate, "This is the price we have to pay, so we will pay it." In a deeper vein it is perhaps also this attitude that made Americans the great soldiers needed for fighting subsequent wars in order to maintain this hard-won freedom.

America has benefited mightily from the immigrants' straightforward attitudes to life's daily problems, including death, and has been strengthened by these stoic attitudes over the sacrifices resulting from wars and disasters. Wailing and lamenting were never viewed as a solution. We honor our lost ones while simultaneously trying to understand the complexity of the causes; at least this has been the case in the past. The lesson learned from our recent 9/11 disaster is not yet evident.

How does the loss of and separation from loved ones contribute to wisdom? An ageless unanswerable question.

For the Askovian immigrants the finality of death was both brutal and accepted. Since these immigrants had experienced separation earlier, they were perhaps a little less distraught than would otherwise have been the case. I was blessed with having two younger sisters. The first was baptized Solveig, which in Danish means sunny road, and by golly she has always been a sunny person, regardless of the adversities she has endured. As a farmer's wife in Iowa she had to be flexible and go with whatever gifts nature gave to farmers. My second sister, Edith, first became a registered nurse and later a college librarian. Her stories about seeing life at its lacerated edges are both humorous and tragic. As young siblings, the three of us had our differences, but the aging process has now pretty well sanded these edges.

Askovian farm life was as dynamic and diverse as the ocean's surf. As a child life seemed to me to be in perpetual motion, with farm chores that changed significantly with each passing season. This state of flux kept one always looking to the future. Reflecting back I believe this is the reason farmers are the most optimistic group of people in the world. The Danish immigrant farmers enjoyed gallows humor. "If you think this year's crops are bad, wait till you see next year's," was a typical remark.

Interestingly enough process and results of farming are analogous to the teaching profession. "If you think this class of students is problematic, just wait till you seen next semester's crop."

I have a poignant recollection of one time (among many), I was complaining about some assigned chore, and exclaimed, "If only I had been born rich," etc. I was quietly, but firmly, told by my immigrant parents that, "If only the dog hadn't stopped to take a shit on the road, it would not have gotten run over, either."

Lesson well learned: "If only" arguments go absolutely nowhere.

This pithy Askovian philosophical approach did serve as an attitude adjustment, and again we see an immigrant trait that has translated into and influenced subsequent American attitudes. "We are each the captains of our destiny, and we'd better not stop to take a shit on the road, unless we wish to be run over."

As the thirties moved toward the forties, Hitler had fully taken over Germany as its dictator and relentlessly begun to grab up huge hunks of Europe. Incredible stories of genocide began creeping into news reports, but tended not to be believed. Surely humans could not do this to each other—or could they? The death of my closest friend had been a singular tragic event, but now the word death was being used to express the loss of thousands.

The immigrant Danish farmers could do little about the conflagration raging in Europe at that time, because too many Americas were isolationists. Indeed, America had not learned its lesson from World War I. There was still some misguided comfort stemming from the fact that we were separated from Europe by an ocean. Askovians, erstwhile Vikings, were relatively ineffective in changing America's isolationist attitude, due to small numbers. The community hunkered down. School and activities related to education become their source of strength. A hell of a lot of sharing went on— socialism at its best. But the issue was openly debated: Why did America not do more to stop Hitler?

The H.C. Andersen School and Lutheran church of the Dancing Danes flourished and became the town's two focal points. Everyone was dirt poor, rock rich, and in some ways proud of it, yet there was no graffiti and certainly no destruction of each other's property. People made their own beer and fruit wines, and shared their meager resources, much as in the sagas of old. The Kettle River Trot was now passé, however. It was wartime, and few were dancing.

These Askovian pioneers founded a fantastic newspaper that everyone subscribed to and read thoroughly. It was called the *Askov American*. It had many of the large city paper features, while including local news, but not in the gossipy manner of a tabloid. Obviously a liberal paper, it always had articles about the school in it. Kids would see their name in print on a fairly regular basis, which of course got them proudly hooked on reading. To this day the *Askov American* is still representing the earlier thirst the immigrants had for information and their need for the kind of communication that is not fulfilled by the electronic media.

The Danish immigrants behaved quite differently in the face of internal frustrations than subsequent generations. Education and culture were given top billing and priority, even in those times of adversity. So what if you had few possessions? You could still have personal dignity, learn to think, have private thoughts, and spice life with humor. Developing and expressing yourself positively were the important things.

Today we sadly witness many personal frustrations expressed in angry cop-killer type of rap songs and the glorified destruction of people's own property and community, e.g., the Watts riot. How in the world did this become acceptable behavior in response to poverty and frustrations? The results of these behaviors have yet to be fully assessed, but we do know that during much of the twentieth century, immigrants and their progeny survived the economically brutal 1930s in relatively good condition, without resorting to self-destruction and defamation. Perhaps this was because during times of hardship, immigrants dedicated themselves to a personally optimistic worldview focused on knowledge and skill development, as opposed to blaming someone else.

Even as life went on in Askov, problems, *big* problems, were not so quietly arising overseas. War had erupted throughout most of Europe and parts of Asia, in spite of statements about "peace in our time." Stories from Asia now rivaled the horror in Europe. Countries throughout Europe had now fallen to the Nazis.

The Germans, for whom the Danes have never had any great love, were now rumored to be doing ghastly things, especially to the Jews. We waited and hoped that the rumors were overblown or false. Mother kept saying the things we heard simply couldn't be true; people do not behave in such an animalistic fashion. We believed her—sort of. But what few photographs were printed belied her optimism, and what little mail got through from the folks throughout Europe indicated that things were gruesome.

Askovian adults openly expressed an aura of uneasiness. America had to get involved in another global conflict—but when?

Our family was now fully committed to rutabagas, cows, chickens, turkeys, and a couple of horses to provide power for tilling the soil. Father had several jobs to provide for his family, so we often did not see him for long periods of time. He had two farms to work, one in the dust bowl of Montana and the other on a rock pile in Minnesota. Odd jobs with the Askov Granary provided much needed hard cash, and the farm produced essential foodstuff.

The future was very uncertain. Small towns throughout America were rapidly becoming restless in the perceived possibility of a global war. The tragic death of my second grade buddy had become a prelude to the hordes of people who were now being slaughtered to satisfy military egomaniacs.

In elementary schools we were learning the "three r's", as well as some raw information about man's inhumanity to each other. Kids across America were facing a reality that their immigrant parents had hoped to protect them from when they left their homelands in search of peace and freedom from oppression.

America's isolationistic complacency during the Great Depression was now extracting its toll. It is my contention, though only a guess, that the immigrants were not the ones leading the march for America's isolationism. These people knew firsthand the political and economic factors that had forced them to leave the very nations that were now in trouble.

Lesson Learned:

Death becomes a sad and incomprehensible personal mystery.

Chapter 8
Rocks and
Rutabagas

While the global political scene was beginning to rage just about everywhere in the world, the Askovian lifestyle continued in a more predictable and somewhat peaceful path. Daily chores, both in the village and on the farm, were essential for survival, and herein lies a secret of the Askovians that is not widely known elsewhere: the Rutabaga.

After having been driven from the dust fields of Montana, my immigrant parents, who neither liked nor succeeded at wheat farming, admitted they had better get on with something else or go hungry. On their arrival in Askov, they were introduced to the long-forgotten prehistoric vegetable called the rutabaga. Indeed, this Stone Age plant had so established itself in Askov, the community was known as:

"The Rutabaga Capital of the World." How embarrassing.

The adult rutabaga is a hard, pasty pale yellow mass, shaped like a child's top, and it tastes great to very hungry cows when chopped up, so they don't have to chew it. It will grow in rocks, on rocks, and under rocks. Genetically this sucker is a supreme survivor in the kingdom of vegetables. Hell, you can't even freeze it in an ordinary refrigerator. The first seed is rumored to have ridden to Askov on an asteroid following the Big Bang. I myself have no doubt it whizzed to Askov on a celestial rock. It truly is a humdinger of a vegetable that must have come from outer edges of our Milky Way galaxy.

When you put the rutabaga into pressurized boiling water for three to four days, it turns into a ghoulish yellow mush that when lavishly doused with "Land o' Lakes" creamy butter and sprinkled liberally with salt, will sustain life for an indefinite period of time—although while it keeps you alive, it may make you wish you could die from hunger. Another little known feature of this delicacy is its universality; people and animals can all eat it with the same degree of dissatisfaction. New Zealanders are especially fond of it, we are told.

Father decided we must, like all the other Askovians, begin raising rutabagas in order for us and the cows to survive. Thereafter the rutabaga chores completely engulfed my otherwise sheltered childhood, dictating daily activities from the cool lengthening frosty days of May until snow mercifully buried them in the shortening, cold wet days of October.

To be modestly successful as a rutabaga farmer, you need to overcome two non-trivial obstacles: one, the rutabaga's own set of growing criteria, and two, the problem of growing them in a rock pile. It was easy to see why people were convinced that rocks and rutabagas had the same origin.

Rocks and rutabagas emerged 14 billion light years ago, when the universe began flying apart and these two suckers successfully clung to one another for dear life. Together they could have attained greatness by becoming a black hole or antimatter, but no, instead they journeyed to Askov.

To farm rutabagas, you must begin with a primitive mindset, just one small notch above our Neanderthal ancestors, by realizing that the rocks must first be removed from the ground where the rutabaga is to grow. For in spite of their cosmic travels, they have not learned to share the same space, so to speak. So early in the morning you grudgingly get out of bed while it is still dark and tromp out to the designated field, contemplating how to clear it of humongous-sized rocks.

As mentioned earlier immigrant Danes have always shown a healthy problem-solving attitude, at least initially. At first they joyfully, with a song in their pulsating hearts, began picking and piling rocks on their property. This varied assortment of rocks became the building blocks of choice for making fences, barns, outhouses, artistic gardens and the like. Askovians quickly realized that since the rocks were free, all you had to do was gather them up and pile them together to become wealthy. What a deal!

This remarkably unproductive gathering process goes on relentlessly in Askov, even today. As one batch of rocks is picked up, another batch belches up from the ground—instantly.

In short, the Great Askovian Rock Pile began eons ago and is destined to continue till the next ice ages, or hell freezes over. Many of the rock piles have been cleverly disguised by the Askovians as fences, so visitors do not steal them. Strange as this behavior may seem to you, dear readers, this practice is working; to date there is no record of any stolen rock piles from Askov. Being a lucky first generation American of spurious Danish Viking background now took on a new meaning as I was instructed to pick and pile rocks, day after day after day. To be a good rock-piler you must be of simple mind, strong back, and hungry.

It goes like this: Your father says, "Son, it is time for you to pick rocks."

"Gawd almighty," you sputter, immediately feeling achy all over, beginning to shake, and throwing yourself on the floor ranting wildly in tongues other than your native Danish.

Father calmly says, in Danish, "That was interesting. I gather you are not hungry today and will not be hungry again until we get the rocks moved."

Your thoughts drift to the Danish word for shit, but you don't dare say it. Instead you get up, dust yourself off, and get ready to pick and pile more rocks.

It should be pointed out that child rearing is a lot easier if you can relate your parental wishes to your child's desire to eat, versus not eating. This distinction clears up any ambiguity a child may have about the value of work. I think there is a truism here that is sometimes missed by the folks who haven't had the experience of being really hungry and seeing no Big Macs on the horizon.

We may ponder why poor people often work for so little—minimum wages. The answer is simple. They are hungry. I am very thankful that I learned this lesson well as a young child. Be assured it was not an easy lesson to learn, but it has certainly helped put things in perspective ever since. This was one of the simplest lessons many boundary layer people have learned:

You must work to eat.

Having made that statement, I have always tried to ensure that my family had plenty of good food, and hunger was never used as a serious paternal motivator to correct their aberrant behavior. Not that it hasn't crossed my mind, however.

On to the chore at hand, piling rocks, which can be studied from a variety of perspectives. Initially you need two tools. First is a heavy, five-foot-long piece of well rusted iron called a crow bar, because you crow a lot when you use it. This abrasive hunk of iron is deftly poked and hammered under the rock designated for relocation.

The second implement is a stone boat. The oxymoronic concept of a stone boat dates back to the early Vikings and is the result of their pitiful attempts at sick humor. It is not a boat at all, and for sure it will not float. It is made from a wooden railroad boxcar door that farmers permanently liberated from the Great Northern or Union Pacific railroads, usually in the dead of night. To the underside of this door are bolted two long medal skids. The device is heavy as sin and totally unsteerable. You attach this homemade contraption to two very strong, fully shackled and dumfounded horses, and call the rig a stone boat. You do not need naval terms like "ahoy" or "shiver me timbers" to operate this non-seafaring vessel.

You now sail, er, drag, your stone boat onto the field containing the rocks your father wants moved. You dig, grunt, curse, and sweat to get the rocks on the boat so they can be relocated as desired. All the while your nervous horses are making distressing grunts, knowing fully what is in store for them. Relieving themselves, as horses often do under stress, gives them momentary relief. But the aroma does not make it any easier for the folks loading rocks on the boat.

Occasionally comes a real treat. There is usually an Askovian farmer in the local area, parts of whose limbs have obviously been left elsewhere. He is the guy with a cache of dynamite, a modern Askovian Viking. He is capable of blowing the shit out of any rock in Askov, given enough TNT. He is truly awesome and greatly admired by teenage males. Females think he is gross, but they don't have to move big rocks, women's lib being still far in the future.

Holding our breath in suspense, we watch this modern boomer dig a hole under the designated rock. In go some sticks of TNT with a short fuse sticking out. Considerable care is given to this process, since dynamite and fuses are expensive and unforgiving once lit.

"Fire in the hole" is the appropriate military expression for detonation, but this Askovian farmer yells either "duck" or "get the hell out of here."

The fuse is carefully lit, and we all dutifully scamper as told, but not too far. We do want to experience some of the explosion's fury. A loud *ka-boom* is heard throughout the countryside, followed by a shower of rocks, dirt, separated gopher body parts, and the like. Danish cheers and cuss words are heard around the field. Good job, Ole!

The fun is quickly over, and we now return to the backbreaking job of gathering up blown rock bits and loading them on the stone boat. The two horses are now rightfully jumpy and skittish. Blinders keep them from seeing where the devastation took place, and they don't like that. But Askovian have learned this truism: Never let your horses face exploding rocks, or you'll never see them again.

Gawd almighty, how we all hated building rock edifices. The fabled Egyptian story about building a cathedral instead of making a rock pile did not persuade any of us to the contrary. The only good news was that when someone later decided to move one of these rock structures, the rocks were at least in a pile, so you didn't have to dig or blow them out again. Ja, for sure, these boundary layer Americans had fun.

Now that enough rocks have been removed, a tiny patch of dirt emerges. It is time to plant rutabaga seeds.

The rutabaga seed, from which comes the bulbous, awkward fiber- and carbohydrate-rich vegetable, is black and very tiny—about the size of the period at the end of this sentence. These little buggers are first planted closely together in rows. They are so close that if not thinned they would simply choke each other to death. Oh yes, my friend, the rutabaga is aggressive beyond belief. To save them from killing each other, farmers produce kids, both sexes, who will do battle with the young and still vulnerable rutabaga.

Father assigns me my weapon for the rutabaga war. It is a three-cornered hoe, generally made from discarded pieces of steel through which is drilled a hole for a bolt that will attach it to a five-foot stick, the hoe's handle. The key to winning the rutabaga-thinning war is to sharpen your three-cornered hoe to a razor's edge. The honing technique requires a file and lots of excess fingers, and no squeamishness about the sight of blood. You get the picture.

The battlefield looks like this: an infinite number

of endless rows of green, vile-looking rutabaga leaves, each about two inches tall. They are leering and challenging you to touch them. The hoe-er's mission is to take his weapon, the hoe, and slowly hoe (chop) his way from one end of the endless row to the other end, leaving a single surviving rutabaga plant every four to six inches.

In this three-dimensional battlefield, rutabagas will hide behind each other to save their own ass. Thus to be a skilled hoe-er, you must alternately push and pull your hoe to successfully leave a single lucky survivor. This job is not for the faint-hearted, but for stupid people with strong backs who will never grow up to become what nature intended them to be. I know this for a fact, because I was destined to be a Lakers center, but because of rutabaga thinning I can now barely get my nose over a bar.

To you psychologists who do research on human beings, rutabaga hoeing would be a fertile field indeed to study the effects of truly boring and inane work. In the hoe-ers mind the infinite number of rows of unhoed rutabagas seem to merge at some vanishing point in the middle of a black hole somewhere in another galaxy, far, far, away. Truly.

Furthermore, as soon as we had hoed the fields on our father's farm, we were rented (slaved) out to farmers who had more fields and/or fewer kids. Askovian slavery was a common practice, and at the time not considered in the least bit inhumane.

Up and down the rows went the hoe-ers, permanently disfiguring their spinal cords, especially the neck and sacroiliac. Talk among us indentured slaves centered on every conceivable topic the mind could dream up to overcome the tedium. No political correctness stuff, just raw politics, dirty sex talk, and sick humor jokes. Sticks and stones can break your bones, but talk can never hurt you—at least not while hoeing rutabagas.

Today at the large universities we are debating "talk free" zones where students can say whatever they wish without fear of retribution. How idiotic. I can't believe how liberated we were to be rutabaga hoe-ers, who for all those years enjoyed a "talk free" zone, up and down the rutabaga rows, in the Rutabaga Capitol of the Whole Damn World.

Few hoe-ers cheated on their tasks. We were goal oriented, seeking only to get to the end of the row so we could sit down, take the pressure off our backbone, drink some tepid water out of a half-gallon tin can that at one time held molasses, and sharpen our hoe. If we were really lucky, we could lie down, stretch out, and dream about flying through the cumulus clouds in the sky. I think it was at this time I developed a strong attachment to flying. Something about "over these prison walls I hope to someday fly."

Since the ground was still supersaturated with rocks, the sharpening of hoes was really only a diversion from working. Any sharp edge gained with great effort was quickly nicked away with the first whack. To this very day the technology of rutabaga hoeing has not changed—that is how advanced it was half a century ago. This is a source of great pride to the Askovian population.

On one of his trips by himself to Montana, Father purchased an enormous tractor. It was a big metal-wheeled monster that belched coal-black stinky smoke and sounded like a dinosaur in heat. Its speed was comparable to a snail crawling toward the dreaded French guillotine. However, its power and sound were comparable to the famous Apollo rocket engines as they roared towards the heavens.

He had the bright idea to have the tractor shipped back to Askov, as the ultimate challenger to the rock-infested fields. It arrived before my dad's return, and while being unloaded broke the skids on the delivery truck and crashed with a loud thump into the muddy ground. The neighbors who had all gathered around to see this behemoth, now deeply mired in mud, howled with laughter.

Soon the unplowed field took on the look of a circus, with onlookers hooting and clamoring, and dogs yowling. This tractor was bigger than the military tanks some of the men knew from WWI. It took the better part of the day to get it righted. Mother was furious that Father wasn't there to muzzle all the merriment and hoopla caused by neighbors.

But once this titan was righted and out of the mud and creeping along, everyone fell at first silent and then applauded triumphantly as it assumed its rightful role of the high tech marvel machine of Askov. It was indeed a defining and proud moment in my childhood. Even Mother's sputtering abated, as she leaked a proud smile. She now had the biggest tractor in town.

I loved this sucker after I got big enough to drive it at about the age of twelve. After my first lumbering solo down a country lane, I really had bragging rights.

The tractor had a huge iron foot petal, called the clutch, three gears forward and one back. It really did not matter which gear you used; they all lumbered along at the same pace. Reverse was a kind of mystery gear, probably designed by a committee of engineers who had varying points of view regarding going backwards. The operator was never sure if it was properly engaged until the clutch was let out and you discovered which direction you were going. The good news was that in reverse it moved very slowly, but the really bad news was you couldn't stop it.

This was not trivial. Backing up was serious business, because the tractor was usually attached to some other device, like a plow, rake or mower. The entire arrangement could dangerously jackknife on you in a misguided reverse maneuver. Father, who did not have a death wish, never really trusted me to do the backing up while he held the hitch of whatever implement needed to be attached. Much better that I hold the hitch, while Father backed up.

Our tractor had only one major limitation. When the ground was hard, dry, or frozen, it was invincible. But when the ground became wet and soft, it simply dug itself a deep, deep hole from which it could not be moved until the ground firmed up by either drought or frost. So you would frequently see the damn thing sitting in odd spots for long periods of time, to the glee of neighbors.

By birthright all farm males qualified for the official Minnesota drivers license when they were big enough to see over the steering wheel and simultaneously reach the wheel and the foot pedals. This was true regardless of mental acumen. You could be, and many were, dumb as stumps and still drive tractors and trucks wherever you wished—at least in Pine County.

Philosophically life at this point had firmly settled into a dull, infinite loop about the futility of being a farmer. Moving from row to row, destroying 99% of the rutabaga seedlings just to allow one to mature, was like playing god of the rutabagas, but this omnipotent power was a bloody joke. Nonetheless, at a gut level, we felt a sense of belonging to the natural process of survival, and we were actively engaged in it daily. This translated into: we would eat for another day. As the twentieth century ran out a couple of years ago, we were faced with the fact that today's children in many parts of the world are facing a far more brutal set of survival conditions than thinning rutabagas.

Today's gang members decide which human being is going to live and which one is to be shot. As Askovian teenagers we only had to decide which rutabaga seedling would be allowed to survive. I do not intend this observation to be smug, but rather as a way to ponder the extreme diversity in what kids do while growing up, then and now.

In order to keep from going mad at the rutabaga-thinning chore, you trained your body to do the work at hand, but freed up your mind to wander and day-dream. You do get to know yourself quite well in this way. I am certain that all people who have very uninteresting and repetitive jobs—assembly lines, sweat shops and the like—must be doing something similar.

What is needed is another federal grant to interview and study these workers and see what kinds of ideas they mentally play with while working at these monotonous jobs. It is possible that they have some very creative ideas that are forever lost in these minds because they have no one to share them with?

Lessons Learned:

There is indeed a devil.

He lives in Askovian rock piles.

He eats rutabagas.

Chapter 9
War & Farming

By the late 1930s and early 1940s, war talk and fear of the future consumed everyone's attention. There was little else to talk about. Reports of events in Europe and Asia were often delayed and inaccurate. Speculation and rumors were thus generated to fill the gaps. The nation was constantly reminded that, "Loose lips sink ships."

Few Askovians had radios, and television was just a laboratory oddity at the time; thus it was only the occasional censored letter from Denmark that gave any clue as to what was happening. Askovian Danes now realized how lucky they were due to their parents' naiveté in buying land, sight unseen, in northern Minnesota. They transformed their gratitude into action to help the struggling family members in Europe.

Askov was indeed fortunate to have its weekly newspaper, the *Askov American*, which came out every Thursday. Hjlmar Petersen, its founder in 1914, ran for governor of Minnesota on the platform that, "Intelligent co-operation between labor, industry and agriculture will be the ultimate solution of our economic difficulties. Government must function to promote that intelligent co-operation." What a vision from a poor immigrant community still suffering from depression and now war!

The first really serious indication that war was imminent in Denmark came when the folks began asking for coffee. You must understand that to a Dane, coffee is more important than their lifeblood. Danish hearts and related arterial plumbing are designed to pump caffeine. So my first clear understanding of shortages resulting from a war was seeing my parents sending as much coffee as they could afford to the old country. Mother kept reminding us that the Danes would survive any calamity, providing they have coffee. Father's favorite comment on how to make coffee was: "save on the water." The brew he made had the consistency of molasses.

As Hitler was rapidly spreading his Nazi evil throughout Europe, the Danish immigrants in Askov knew that it was only a short time before Denmark would be invaded, which happened in April 1940. I clearly remember the day. Our farm worker and I were repairing rusted wire fencing and rotted fence posts.

The hired man's name was Peder Christensen, a true tough Viking roustabout who had long before fallen on hard times. He was elderly, with no family, no source of income other than day jobs, and no visible teeth, only protruding roots that were always infected and caused him great pain, especially in cold weather. To ease the aching in his jaw, he would gnaw on his hands, claiming this helped by shifting the pain from his rotten teeth to his fist. Never once did he complain—about anything. In spite of all his problems, he was an optimistic immigrant who relished his freedom—his most precious possession.

Peder was in his seventies when the German storm troopers invaded Denmark, and the colorful language he used regarding this event was a real education. He so wanted to take a pitchfork and do one-on-one battle with the Nazi monsters. Reports of how all the Danes wore yellow armbands when the Nazis ordered the Jews to do so made us all proud. Accounts of how the daring Danes successfully smuggled Jews across the Oresund Strand to Sweden at night to avoid deportation became a source of satisfaction. At least something was being done to stem the holocaust sweeping Europe.

Patriotism was now running feverishly high. Every teenage Askovian male wanted to join the military service more than anything. We hoped that the war would last until we grew old enough to enlist, while our parents prayed it would not. Several junior and senior high school students, by fudging ages, did make it into the military. They figured this was their opportunity to swap rocks and rutabagas for an unknown experience.

Askov, always a united community, now took on a military resolve. Everyone who was eligible enlisted, and farmers grew rutabagas at an all-time pace, assuming rutabagas were the health elixir of great warriors. Scrap metal was collected by the ton, hauled to town, and piled up along the railroad track spurs for rail transfer to smelters.

Saving everything that could possibly help the war effort became the Askovian mission and a way of life. Everyone was involved in the war effort, and this produced a strong sense of belonging to a higher order. Even the children exchanged what few coins they earned from doing chores for stamps that ultimately became war bonds.

The Japanese attack on Pearl Harbor on December 7, 1941 became the spark that finally inflamed us all and put an end to talk of isolationism. For some it was almost a relief that now, finally, America would stand and be counted.

The attack altered everything we did in our "coming of age in Askov," from daily farming chores to school curricula. Young men were leaving the farms to enter the military. The usual "fun" school activities were stifled by the constant knowledge that people were being slaughtered and that we too would soon be marching to war. The silliness that today's teens enjoy in growing up was not to be part of our youth. Everything was serious and all too often sad.

Making a living as well as contributing to the war effort was a task everyone in the immigrant communities accepted without question. The rationing of gas and sugar were taken in stride, and few cheated. It was not the thing to do.

At this time it became evident that the immigrants had not totally abandoned their roots. To us boundary layer kids, it was a revelation to see how our immigrant parents unselfishly turned to helping those they had earlier left behind.

As an aside, Americans still witness immigrants' devotion to supporting families in the nations they came from by sending goods and monies. This activity has not been adequately recognized or appreciated for is its value as a stabilizing force among nations. The number of people throughout the world that these efforts help is unknown, but the practice has surely eased a lot of suffering and created an admiration for America. This is another illustration of a way immigrants' contributions go unnoticed and unappreciated.

On Askovian farms the animals tended to control all schedules and budgets. At times they were also a source of emotional concern for the children who worked with them. For example, the best meals farm families ever enjoyed were summertime Sunday dinners with fried chicken, new buttery potatoes, and fresh golden corn on the cob. What could be better, after hearing lofty thoughts from an energetic Dancing Dane Lutheran preacher, than coming home to such a feast?

These spring fried chickens did taste good, but I always had a philosophical problem while eating them, since often I was the one who had helped get them to our plates. The baby chicks were cute, fuzzy, and friendly early in the spring. Chicks would actually eat corn out of our hands; they were not afraid. Stupid chickens they were, but somehow, to a kid, they still seemed to possess some kind of personality.

As the chicks and I got older, it became my duty to catch one, take a hatchet, and separate the chicken from its head. The headless body was then tossed into some grass to thrash around as its tiny blood supply drained into the soil, thereby completing its shortened life cycle on planet earth. It was not a pretty sight and a chore I distinctly remember wishing someone else would do. Thankfully my father felt my concerns and frequently did perform the task.

Let me assure you that the proverbial statement, "running around like a chicken with its head cut off" never really struck me as funny, having seen it happen in real life. After the beheading I would put the feathered carcass into a bucket of boiling water to loosen its feathers. Finally my former little playmate would go to Mother, who fixed it up for the tasty Sunday dinner. Not easy, dear reader, but that is life and death on the farm.

These food-providing experiences, essential as they were, did have an effect on my understanding not to waste food. This was not only an economic matter; waste was also viewed as killing more than was really needed. Interestingly enough most animals in the wild do not kill for sport. They just kill enough to eat and no more. Today, as I see kids toss half of their Big Mac lunches in the trash, a certain uneasy feeling arises. Some of those cows were slaughtered just to be thrown away—they were wasted for no good reason at all.

A hungry world must not tolerate waste.

Every farmer had at least one dog for the sole purpose of providing noise when there was an intruder. Kids' bedtime stories about dogs taking good care of innocent wayward sheep while they slept did not square with the lifestyle of our dog, Fido. Fido was the meanest concoction of protoplasm ever created.

Most farm dogs would spend their day lying along a dirt roadway, and when a vehicle came by they would chase it and bark. But not Fido. This mutt dog had the most incredible jaw, with sharp, strong teeth. He would come at a car as though shot from a cannon and try to rip off a tire in one clean bite. It was quite entertaining to lie in the grass and watch Fido attack Mr. Goodyear's finest.

One day, my neighbor boyhood friend Harold and I heard that if you take a chicken, place it on its back, and slide a straw under its feathers so the straw touches the neck skin, the chicken will lie completely still on its back forever. We found it worked, so we soon had the entire front yard covered with chickens lying motionless on their back. We called Mother. She came running to see what had happened to her poultry, which was a major source of family cash flow and food supply.

Mother was not particularly impressed or disturbed by the sight of her chickens lying with their feet straight in the air. She merely grunted and immediately kicked the nearest chicken. The straw was dislodged, and the hen ran off merrily squawking and clucking. Mother continued to kick the chickens while we sat there laughing our heads off, talking about my mother's ability to perform miracles.

The automobile was rapidly emerging throughout the land as both a necessity and a symbol of American freedom, even though cars were very difficult to get during the war years. Ford and his assembly plant concept had, prior to the war, produced countless Model Ts and As. The assembly plant idea was now turning out planes and boats to meet the war needs. Everyone dreamed of someday having his or her own auto. For the immigrant, having a car was the ultimate achievement—probably still is for many.

Nearby lived an elderly immigrant couple by the name of Hassenfelt. They were content with their horses for pulling power and transportation, and were not really hooked on the idea of auto ownership. But it finally happened. Mr. Hassenfelt got an old used Model T Ford, which from the get-go gave him no end of trouble. A modern-day Askovian Luddite, he frequently complained that this kind of technology was going to be the ruin of good Askovian farming.

He kept his Ford in an unheated shed during the winter, where it would naturally freeze up. Antifreeze or alcohol was far too expensive. If he had gotten hold of alcohol, he probably would have drunk it anyhow.

One frosty winter morning the frozen car problem again presented itself. Mr. Hassenfelt decided to heat up his car before trying to start it. He got some oily rags, put them in a flat pan, poured kerosene over it, torched the mixture, and shoved the flaming mess under his Model T.

While allowing time for his car to warm up, he went into his house to have another cup of coffee with his beloved bride of fifty-plus years. The next thing the neighborhood heard was a loud *ka-boom* as the roof of Hassenfelt's shed separated from the building, his Model T engulfed in flames accompanied by billowing black clouds of smoke.

The unflappable Mr. Hassenfelt came strolling out of his house, cup of coffee in hand, and stoically watched the conflagration, all the while adding colorful Danish remarks to the effect that he guessed his car was now warm enough. With a shrug he walked back into his house to his waiting wife for another cup of coffee, muttering that he never really liked that Model T anyhow. With it gone, tomorrow would be a better day. And so he let the mess burn itself out.

We giddy frozen spectators admired this kind of spirit and hoped that someday we, too, could face adversity with the same aplomb. Indeed, many times since this experience have I wished for Mr. Hassenfelt's demeanor. As the country western song goes, "You got to know when to fold 'em," and Mr. Hassenfelt sure did.

Many of these elderly Askovians ate nothing but butter, eggs fried in butter, rutabagas cover with butter, and pork fat, and often capped off meals with a plug of chewing tobacco. Yet they seemed to live forever. Could it be that their uncanny ability to handle the tribulations of everyday stress kept them alive, and nutrition has little to do with anything? Their indomitably strong dreams and hopes, well seasoned with humor, controlled their bodies.

By 1944 the reports from Europe and Asia raised hope that the slaughtering would end with the Allies the victors. This hope did not do much to lighten the constant reports of losses. Many had relatives or friends who were in combat and losing their lives. I had a cousin, a medical doctor, who was stuck in Denmark, although he was an American. He managed to get out and back to New York City. His father, my uncle, got to spend only a few days with him before he was shipped off again. He was on the American troop ship *Dorchester* when a German U-boat torpedoed it in the frigid North Atlantic. This was the ship on which chaplains from three different faiths stood together as the vessel sank.

In spite of the war still raging around the world, our teenage years were nonetheless characterized by normal hormonal shifts—male gonads sinking closer to the center of the earth and female bodies magically beginning to attract the males' attention. We had few school dances, social events, or parties, as the worldwide tragedy weighed heavily on all our school activities.

On the farm, however, there was always plenty of sex. In order for the animals to produce the products we needed, they were encouraged to be sexually active. Initially the farm sex business was titillating, but it actually became a bore when you found yourself trying to hold a cow steady while the bull had his jollies, especially in slippery snow-covered barnyards in the dead of winter. Cows seemed to be in heat only when it was cold outside, a little known fact outside of Askov. But without this event there would be no calves and no future cows to milk and eat.

About this time Father started taking a University of Minnesota extension course on artificial insemination and invited me to go along. This procedure was something quite new for its day. It spelled bad news for the bull, but its intent was to improve the herd. Most Askovian farmers had no interest in interfering with nature's way, but dear Dad did—if we could make another buck off the milk cows.

The essential ingredient is harvested from the bull and mixed with egg albumin, kept warm, and then with the help of a glass tube—a pipette—and a penlight, the mixture is transferred into the right spot in a cow at the right time. This probably sounds simple; however, there are many potential areas where this system can fail.

As the insemination is taking place, the poor cow is making gutteral moaning noises, perhaps grieving for her bull friend who must have died, since there is no excited bull making his ranting orgasmic racket. Now all that passes for romance are just some simple farm blokes quietly discussing politics. The inseminator and Dad proceed, always ending with the statement, "I sure hope this works." I had the funny feeling, probably like the absent bull, "Oh, shit, is this what sex is finally coming to?" This farmyard sex had until this time had two dimensions; an emotional/physical component, which was rapidly being lost, and an economic consequence that was taking over. Interestingly this was to become a harbinger of today's cloning activities. Human sexual activity is still viewed as enjoyable experiences, but the product of these encounters can now be manipulated, hopefully for the better.

The Great War—what an oxymoronic term—in

Europe finally ended in June of 1945. The miseries that had accompanied it were beginning to be tallied up, and the results were grotesque. Furthermore, there was still a nasty mess in Asia that seemed to portend an incredible slaughter as an invasion of Japan was being anticipated.

Lessons Learned:

Wartime childhood is not much fun.

We must strive to prevent future confrontations,

not for ourselves,

but for the sake of all kids.

Chapter 10
Your Horse Needs an Enema

"Your horse needs an enema" was one of the strangest comments I had ever heard at a noontime Viking dinner table, a time of day that city folk call lunch. Genteel Askovian farmers ate dinner at noon and supper at night.

As I earlier remarked upon, the immigrant farmers possessed a unique set of problem-solving skills that often surreptitiously included wry humor. I was now about to learn that these immigrants also had some innate veterinarian skills, or so they believed.

Ja, sure, here goes.

Near high-noon dinnertime one cold and wet windy fall day, the farmers were helping each other to collectively bring in the fruits of their earlier summer labor. The horses on that particular day were pulling flatbed wagons loaded with bundled corn stalks that now had to be chopped up and blown into a silo. Picking up dried corn stalks, with their razor-sharp, muddy leaves, was no picnic, and dinner was always a much anticipated respite, a time to eat, rest, and clean up wounds.

At a neighbor's farmhouse, the farmers tromped in, washed up, and sat around a large wooden dining table. The cat was the first one on the table and nonchalantly dragged its fluffy tail through the gravy bowl. The lady of the house was nonplused. She simply grabbed the cat's nape with her left hand, and with her right thumb and forefinger deftly squeezed the gravy from the cat's tail back into the bowl. Then she tossed the cat off the table.

My father and I witnessed this smoothly orchestrated salvage maneuver, momentarily speechless. Then Dad patted my shoulder and with a twinkle in his eye whispered, "Go easy on the gravy, son".

Several of the other farmers who had also seen this gravy recovery episode decided to go light on their gravy helpings as well and were trying to find something to say or do so as not to attract attention.

As food was passed around, farmer style, the lady of the house kept asking why weren't we taking more gravy. After all, she had just made it. No one wanted to answer her directly. So to tactfully defuse the situation one of the farmers began to complain loudly from the far side of the table that one of his horses wasn't pulling its fair share of the load.

Several farmers smiled knowingly at each other and began expressing their concern, relieved to get off the gravy caper and continue eating. This was when another creative farmer suggested it was enema time for the malingering horse. I simply could not believe the ensuing discussion. These farmers were suddenly serious! Problem solving, which was their mettle, had again captivated their attention to the exclusion of everything else. They were focused.

The poor lady of the manor who had prepared and served the meal was still sputtering about her unpopular gravy, but was completely ignored. Serious matters were now on the table. Seemed that every farmer had at one time or another had a similar experience with one of his horses. Theories on workhorses, along with anatomical explanations, were being wildly described and debated as if every farmer had graduated from vet school. The creative farmer who had initially brought up his horse's lethargic behavior now himself began to believe that his horse did indeed need some attention.

Finally, a general consensus arose around the dinner table, just as dessert and coffee were being served. The low-performing horse was definitely showing signs of constipation and was in dire immediate need of an enema.

"Pass the sugar and cream for my coffee, please," said the farmer with the ailing horse. "We must do what has to be done", ja sure.

The horse had now unwittingly become the sacrificial animal for a house cat's lack of good table manners.

Next came a series of poorly thought-out theories about how to physically perform the procedure—there being no web pages available. I observed in disbelief as we all became seriously engaged as a committee to arrive at a workable plan. Today's university departments could have learned a lesson on procedures in conducting faculty meetings if they had only been present in this humble Askovian farmhouse with a supposedly stuffed-up horse in the barn.

Dessert over, everyone moved on to the barn, where the happy, unsuspecting hay-munching horse was put into a stall. The horse was given some additional hay to further soothe him while preparations were in progress. I certainly could not discern any horse constipation behavior from the way he merrily continued chewing. Boy oh boy, was he in for a surprise.

The farmers were devising a plan as they went along. The agreed-upon mission was to somehow encourage the horse to relieve himself so he would pull his wagon more expeditiously that afternoon. A couple of the farmers expressed a real interest in the outcome of this procedure, as they, too, felt they had horses that were not pulling their fair load.

"Ja, now vait yust a minute, boys," says the farm owner. "Ve haven't got enough time to give all your horses enemas this afternoon. Ve have got to get the silo filled vith corn before it spoils rotten."

A six-foot stepladder was placed behind the horse's rear end, upon which the enema-or would stand. (Definitions: horse is the enemee, farmer is the enemor.) A long piece of thick gasoline hose, about two inches in diameter, was procured from an abandoned gas tank and lathered with axle grease; you can guess why. A gasoline funnel was placed in one end of the hose. With all the mechanical implements now in place, practice was about to meet theory.

Meanwhile another team of farmers had been cooking up two buckets of hot soapy lye water. The question of temperature was widely discussed to ensure it was not too hot. Wrists and elbows were used as thermometers.

The horse was still contently munching his hay, completely unaware of what was shortly to befall him. Innocence is bliss.

Since I was small it was decided I would get on top

of the ladder and pour the soapy water into the funnel. Then, mercifully, they decided I was too small, so it would be best for me to stand up front and watch the horse.

All the elements were go for launch. A farmer mounted the stepladder, while concurrently the greased gas hose was inserted into the horse's nether parts by another farmer and his buddy.

I was looking into the horse's eyes, which suddenly grew large as saucers and began rolling rapidly, one clockwise, the other counterclockwise.

Launch time. The farmer on top of the ladder began to pour hot soapy water into the wide end of the funnel, where it made its way to the other end of the hose, deep within the horse's private parts.

Anatomically the horse's nervous system was energized into chaos as signals from its rectum and colon sped to its medulla oblongata, the part of the brain that is in charge of all horses', as well as man's, emergencies. All the elements of the horse's nervous system were now engaged and enraged as panic survival messages were sent to his muscular and skeletal systems. The horse let out a death-defying roar and reared up on its front feet. This was biology in action, and I was seeing it firsthand.

As the business of this medical procedure now rapidly unfolded, the unlucky farmer holding the funnel on top of the ladder and his buddy with the bucket of hot water on the stool were catapulted into the back of the barn by the flailing hind legs of the over-stimulated horse.

In less than a nanosecond, the hot soapy water containing lots of horsy green stuff was jetted out of the horse and splattered over the rearward positioned farmers and throughout the barn.

Loudly cheering pandemonium set in as the poor, bewildered and formerly constipated horse whinnied his discontentment. The green stuff that generously coated the rear-positioned farmers made them look like screaming beanstalks. The uninvolved, but objective observers, including myself, were beside ourselves with laughter.

The key farmers in this medical drama, expressing real and imagined wounds, ran aimlessly around, damning and cursing in a Danish dialogue that I clearly understood. The horse, now slowly recovering its composure, continued its loud eruptions, to the consternation of the farmer who owned the building.

Ja, for sure, now comes the blame part. "Whose cockamamie idea was this anyhow?" And, "You are all going to have to help me clean up this mess." My sides hurt more from laughing than did the unlucky twits who got kicked in the ribs.

That afternoon, the medically treated horse literally dragged his teammate around the cornfield at lickety-split speed. Every time someone so much as looked at him, he would produce a wide grin, assuring us that he was indeed cured.

Debates continued for years as to whether or not this horse really was in need of so much attention. The only certain consolation to this episode on this cold wet dreary October day was that we all got out of eating gravy stirred by a cat's tail.

I know for sure that the creative farmers who suggested this treatment are still trying to get their work published in the horsy medical journals.

Lessons Learned:

Watch what you eat.

Always pull your fair share of the load.

Chapter 11
The Frailty of Dickey

The frailty of Dickey is a special chapter, because it illustrates a relationship between children and animals. Indeed, all life on earth may be woven more interdependently than we yet realize.

In spite of the poverty of the immigrant Askovian farmers, they were most generous in helping those less fortunate than themselves, especially children. This behavior is seen throughout most immigrant communities, especially poor ones. Perhaps their sense of vulnerability fosters this cooperative spirit. They help each other and anyone else they feel is in need.

For several summers my folks would adopt children from an orphanage in Chicago. This gave these kids a few months of freedom from the cramped, miserable quarters that had become their home while they waited to be permanently adopted. Farmers were especially sought after as hosts, since this gave the kids an opportunity to experience the wide out-of-doors and to be with animals.

One of these summers was to become indelibly etched in all our memories. A youngster of about seven

or eight, by the name of Dickey, came to us in late June
after his school was out. He was a good-looking lad
with a pleasant, though sad smile. Everything was fine,
except he did not talk. He would not verbally respond
to any question. He never asked for anything, and he
was always obedient to whatever was required of him.
The information my mother had received was that he
had been severely abused and now would simply not
talk—to anyone.

What to do?

Father decided to give Dickey a kitten, of which
we had many; the barn was full of them. The instruction to Dickey included that he was to be totally in
charge of this animal. He could play with it, he could
sleep with it, and he was to keep it fed. This was now
Dickey's kitten. Initially he was not sure just what to
do, never having had an animal before, but he took good
care of it, and the two became inseparable. He would
cart it around with him by day, and they would curl up
together at night.

Lo and behold, one day Dickey started saying a few
words. Our parents told us not to pay undue attention,
but continue to talk to him like we would anyone else.
Time passed, and soon Dickey was chattering away like
any other normal kid his age. He had a good vocabulary, and he knew when to yell and when to speak softly.

This amply proved to me the power that animals
can have in people's lives. The incident became quite a
conversation piece in the community, where everyone
knew what everyone else was doing every second.

Come August, soon it would be time for Dickey to
return to Chicago. It was also time to harvest corn, chop
it up, and put it in silo storage for use later in the winter. Farmers did this in a collective way; they would help

each other and move from farm to farm until everyone's work was done. The day came for them to "fill the silo" at our home. A half dozen tractors pulling flatbed trailers would haul in the bound corn stalks, which were then hand shoved into a tractor-driven silo-filler machine. The silo-filling machine sliced the corn into small pieces and blew it up into the top of the silo. The contraption was noisy as hell and dangerous.

The corn harvest was a very busy time for the farmers. Winter would soon be setting in, which could mean rain and even snow flurries. No time to waste.

At mid-morning, Dickey, his kitten, and I were standing watching this operation with the cacophony of tractors whizzing around and the silo filler's whining slicing blades. Suddenly Dickey's cat was frightened and bounded from his clutches, to be ground in the mud by the huge rear tires of a fast-moving tractor. It was all over in an instant—the kitten squashed beyond recognition.

Dickey quietly turned away and hurried into the house to his room, where he lay down on his bed. I tried to get his attention, but to no avail.

From that moment, Dickey again fell mute, like the day he arrived almost three months earlier. He did not talk to any of us for the rest of the summer, which was only a couple of weeks. He obeyed, nodded, and functioned, but never spoke or smiled for us again. We tried everything, but the grief from the loss of his kitten was too great for him to understand and overcome. Another kitten was not the answer. He had apparently re-experienced an incident comparable to what had made him go mute initially.

Needless to say this was a real bummer for us all. The episode touched the entire Askovian community that throughout the summer had participated in Dickey's metamorphosis from a mute to a normal kid and now back into his cocoon. The unfortunate young driver of the tractor was devastated. Collectively we cried and tried everything possible to reach Dickey once again.

I was just a teenager then, but the incident left an indelible impression. Later, when I became a teacher and when faced with a problem student, I would frequently be jerked back to my memories of Dickey.

Many years later, when taking groups of teachers to visit and study alongside teachers in Scandinavia, we came across a program in Copenhagen where the public school actually ran a small farm in the city with a wide variety of animals. Problem students in the Copenhagen School system were encouraged to adopt animals at this farm for a period of time. If the animals were small enough—chickens, rabbits, and the like—they could take them home for some of the time. For larger animals like horses, cows, and pigs, the students had to come to the farm every day to tend to their adopted animals.

It was amazing and heartwarming to walk through this farm and see kids sitting, petting and talking to their animal friends. These often disturbed and abused kids simply seemed to know what to do and how to communicate with the animals. I am sure there is a message here in the raising of humans, especially those who are lonely and have been mistreated.

Danish school counselors said this program was a huge success for troubled kids; some went so far as to suggest that all inner city schools, which by their nature are isolated from rural areas, should have an animal farm where kids who do not have pets can be exposed to a variety of domesticated animals.

Visiting one of today's super-sterile zoos, like the famous one in San Diego, California, is absolutely no substitute for having an animal that a child can handle, pet, and whisper sweet nothings to. Petting zoos are a good beginning, but perhaps for some kids a real kitten of their own is better. It had certainly done wonders for Dickey.

Yes, children are frail.

Teachers, parents, and community members must be ever vigilant to not push kids too far or too fast. The flip side is we must also not always give in to their begging whims simple to relieve some momentary stress. This can be a tight rope to walk. But cruelty is never acceptable behavior.

There is some good news. Mother did keep in touch with the orphanage, and Dickey did grow up. He served his country in the U. S. Army and later became a policeman in Chicago. But his childhood had surely been a challenging one.

How many kids are there throughout the world whose lives secretly harbor unfathomable fears and abuses? Some will overcome these horrifying experiences, others will not, and still others will themselves become monsters who perpetuate more grief.

Tragically much of this abuse comes from parents, social services, and even our religious institutions—the very agencies that kids respect and look to for love, sustenance and guidance.

Lessons Learned:

Do not underestimate the frailty of a little abused boy.

Do not underestimate the healing power of a little kitty.

Chapter 12
Ecstasy of Flying

As the intensity of the war increased, the pilots in the American Air Corps became everyone's heroes. All this teenager and his classmates dreamed of doing was flying fighters and bombers, and we constantly talked about it. Accounts of our heroes' experiences taking place in the real world, like Jimmy Doolittle's "Thirty Seconds over Tokyo"; Scott's experiences with the Flying Tigers; flying the hump over China in "God is My Co- Pilot"; and the island fighting in "Guadalcanal Diary" made for exciting reading and served as dramatic incentives for us to become avid readers in school. Of course the conditions of the times made all the students in H.C. Andersen School seek the printed word—there was no TV.

We studied the specifications and performance statistics of the various airplanes in depth, to the satisfaction of our teachers. Suddenly mathematics and sciences courses, which until the war we had viewed as rather mundane subjects, now became exciting. All the scientific concepts involved with aviation took on new and poignant meaning.

The force of gravity was especially exciting, since it involved dropping objects from high places. It is amazing how important knowledge can become to kids when there seems to be a reason for knowing it. At that time, the speed of sound was viewed as a barrier that would remain impenetrable. Energy and power became topics of animated discussions, along with the formulas that defined them. Once, we even got hold of some old military manuals that presented these topics in more exciting ways than our textbooks.

Events of such magnitude as the Second World War, the Russian launching of Sputnik, and the United States landing a man on the moon have done more for American math and science education than all the reform movements in history. Tragically, many schools did not effectively use these events to enhance classroom education. Education that is disconnected from the real world impedes good learning.

My favorite plane throughout the war was the "forked-tailed" P-38 Lightning. To me this plane represented the ultimate fighting machine—heavy armor, two powerful Allison inline engines, reasonably maneuverable, with a shape that was certainly futuristic. The P-51 Mustang was a close second.

Near the end of the war it became possible to buy balsa wood kits to build your own models of many of these fighters and bombers. The models were not cheap, around four bits (fifty cents) or so. But somehow I was able to get my hands on a few which I cherished until leaving home.

First came the breathtaking moment of unpacking and carefully cutting out the preprinted thin balsa pieces that would later be glued together to make the P-38 skeleton. Those of you who have enjoyed building models know how truly frustrating the cutout process can be, especially with a dull one-edged razor blade. Your cut often goes too far, nipping your finger in the process, and now you have to re-glue the over-cut pieces together and wipe off your blood. At this time few thought anything of the fact that kids really, *really* liked to use the sticky clear glue that came in a squeeze tube. Gluing was an especially enjoyable part of building models because it smelled so good. We had no idea that it was making us buzz around mentally; indeed, adults would often come in and ask if they could have a sniff. We certainly did not know then how distressing and damaging this glue-sniffing issue was to become.

In the early forties, when the war was thankfully beginning to show signs that we would win, at least in Europe, other peacetime activities slowly began to infiltrate our daily lives. One day a single-engine plane, a J-3 Piper Cub that had been used for training pilots and then discarded, came to town and was offering rides out of a farmer's field for two bucks. I was about fourteen and totally committed to becoming a fighter pilot. I don't remember how, but I managed to get two bucks without my parents knowing about it. I did not steal the money—I don't think.

Off I went to the hayfield where this daring aviator was skinning people a couple of bucks for a short flight. What a sight. The pilot was sitting regally in the front seat of his red-fabric-coated J-3 Piper Cub with large numbers painted on the wings. He was wearing the famous Ray-Ban sunglasses—but no scarf.

Shaking with excitement I forked over the two bucks and asked about a parachute. He said it would not be necessary, since we would not be doing acrobatics for two dollars. Darn! I climbed aboard, and for the first time in my life I clipped on a seat belt and shoulder harness, which made me feel *very* important.

The pilot yelled "contact," and his buddy started to manually turn the propeller. Suddenly, with a distinct *pop,* the engine fired and belched a sooty cloud of black smoke. The Cub was loud indeed, since the planes had practically no muffler. The pilot moved the joystick and kicked the pedals on the floor while revving up the engine.

Slowly, and at first softly, we began moving downwind across the newly mowed gopher-holed and rock-infested hayfield. At the end of the field, he turned the J-3 Cub into the wind and applied full power. The engine roared, and now I could clearly see through the prop. Bumpity-bump we headed down the rough meadow. The noise was now deafening, and the machine felt as if it would fall apart. Slowly the tail began to rise, and I could see straight out front.

What a magnificent sight! For sure, this was the fastest I had ever gone. The trees beside the field were passing by very fast now; however, the trees at the end of the field were coming into view with equal speed. *Will we make it?* Slowly we began to lift, but each time it got off the ground the plane settled back down, then bounced back up again. The bumps were getting farther apart, and finally we bumped no more.

This was absolutely the greatest moment in my life up to that time. I was flying! The tickle in my stomach, the view in my eyes, the sound in my ears and the smell of exhaust fumes were simply overpowering.

As a kid, there is absolutely no experience like your first small airplane ride.

Sensing my enthusiasm the pilot turned around and told me to take the famous joystick, put my feet on the pedals, and see if I can fly. Luckily I had built a model of a plane's controls and had practiced with it in our barn, so I knew a little bit about the way the controls were suppose to behave. He did not have to make that offer twice.

It was unbelievable! Here I was, actually making the plane turn, go up, and go down. The pilot was most generous in letting me fly without interfering with the controls, except that I was not allowed to touch the throttle. The urge was to dive!

What a magnificent view opened before me, of the long lines of rutabagas growing straight as an arrow in the fields below. We had done a good job of hoeing, and now we were flying over the lush green rows. Wow. Even though our speed was only about 75 mph and we were up just a few hundred feet, the experience was overwhelming.

It seemed like only a few moments before we headed back down for the landing. Even as the little plane began to flare in preparation for settling back to earth, my heart kept up its rapid beat. Finally we stalled for a bumpy landing on the meadow. My first flight had ended. *Damn.*

My early experiences of jumping off haystacks with the turkeys had finally paid off. I was now the only lucky student in the H.C Andersen High School who had actually had a plane ride. I was hooked on flying forever—but out of money.

Almost half a century later, fortune would allow

me to fly an Air France Concorde jet from Rio de Janeiro to Paris via Senegal. But this SST ride, even at Mach 2.04 (1500 miles per hour) at 60,000 feet and drinking an endless supply of Dom Perignon champagne, in no way compared to the utter thrill of that first Piper Cub ride from an Askovian hayfield in my early teens.

Flying is one of those experiences that touch each of us land-based mortals in a different way. You have to feel especially sorry for those poor souls who are so frightened of flying that they never fully enjoy the experience. The "white knucklers" should have early in life hoed rutabagas in rocky fields.

For me, true excitement would be to take a shuttle flight and see our blue planet from outer space. Since we now have the skills and the experience, these trips into the cosmos will surely become common practice for many in the near future.

An immigrant father busted prairie sod with oxen, and his boundary-layer kid rode in a Concorde and can realistically envision a space ride. Wow. These unprecedented advances could only happen in America—all thanks to our immigrants.

Lesson Learned:

If there is reincarnation,

try to come back as a bird.

Chapter 13
The Atomic Age Cometh

The war in Europe ended May 7, 1945 at 2:41 AM in Reims, France. Surrender took place in a little red schoolhouse, which had been Eisenhower's headquarters. Now came an accounting of the unbelievable horror that Europe had been undergoing. The revelations from the military tribunals that were to follow gave our species little to be proud of, except that somehow some of us had emerged from a period of great darkness and were again trying to bring order out of chaos.

America's and its Allies' military losses in Asia were still mounting with no end in sight. The photos and movies coming back from the island wars showed incredible brutality. Projections of the number of soldiers to be lost in the anticipated invasion of mainland Japan were unthinkable.

The Japanese warriors were being profiled in the media as the meanest sons-a-bitches the world had ever seen. Their beastly behavior against civilians throughout Asia had for sure earned them that title. The Japa-

nese military leaders showed little inclination toward
forsaking their notorious historical background under
the shoguns. Futile suicide efforts became revered hero-
ism.

**Today the world is again witnessing this
dreadful behavior – especially among the
young - why?**

Spring 1945 - it seemed to many of us that America
was experiencing more dread about the consequences
of the impending final fight with the Japanese than we
had felt over the Normandy invasion of Europe.

Discussions on the H.C. Andersen campus were
most depressing. Those of us who were in our mid teens
were certain we would see action in the looming invasion of Japan. Our social studies teacher, a former naval aviator who had been wounded on the Yorktown
off Midway Island in 1942, spent countless hours talking with us and telling us how horrible it is to see flames
consume your colleagues as your ship explodes and
sinks.

In July of 1945 I was fortunate enough to attend a
one-week summer camp at Grand View College in Des
Moines, Iowa. This came about largely because my
Uncle Joe was the president and helped me get funds to
go. He was a brilliant logician, enjoyed science as an
avocation, and was full of energy. We had always shared
good conversations, and he taught me a lot when I was
a kid.

E = mc². This simple equation was about to became part of our daily vocabulary— though we had few clues as to what it was going to mean.

Albert Einstein, a superb mathematician and scientist, had suddenly become a household name. But what had he and his colleagues really said and done and what did it mean?

Past historical efforts to transmute lead to gold would pale next to this simple relationship stating that matter could be transformed into energy. We heard news reports of a possible new weapon, based on this knowledge, of such destructive capabilities that it might destroy the entire world if it were ever detonated. What was it, and who had it, and what should be done with it?

Uncle Joe, formally GVC President Johannes Knudsen, had studied at the University of Copenhagen prior to World War II, when the physicists Niels Bohr and Werner Heisenberg were also there. After the beginning of WW II, all anyone knew was that Professor Bohr had sided with the Americans and his former student, Heisenberg, had gone south to Germany. While Danish Bohr did work on the highly secret American Manhattan Project, it is not known exactly what Heisenberg accomplished for Germany with his heavy water experiments for the Nazis in Norway. The two men had a meeting in 1941, the content of which is still unknown. Speculations over this encounter later became the subject of a fascinating play called *Copenhagen*.

The Manhattan Project was rumored to be trying to convert mass into pure energy and was viewed as a scientific holy grail. The mathematics of such a transformation indicated a staggering amount of energy would result. The process, called nuclear fission, relies on splitting atoms of selected elements, producing an enormous release of energy. The theory is relatively simple, but the procedures to do the splitting are extremely difficult. The idea of getting this all into a deliverable device, i.e., a bomb, was thought by many to be remote.

This scientific challenge, code named the Manhattan Project, is a classic example of the "can do" attitude that exemplifies America. It was an incredible cooperative effort.

The project was successful thanks to the influence and cooperation of immigrants, many of whom were not even citizens. They had been granted refuge as the war clouds were gathering over Europe during the 1930s.

Mid morning of July 16, 1945, while playing a softball game, my Uncle Joe came to find me at our camping area on the Grand View College campus. He told me that, as predicted, an atomic device, a precursor to the bomb, had that morning been detonated in the New Mexico desert at Alamogordo. It was called Trinity.

The news was most sobering, even to us pimple-faced teenagers. Our game stopped abruptly as everyone wanted to know more about what had happened; our campfire was somber that night. We had entered the atomic age and didn't have a clue what it meant. We only knew we felt icy fear.

President Truman and Prime Minister Attllee, recent successor to Churchill as Prime Minister of England, called for Japan to surrender or suffer catastrophic consequences. The Japanese warlords ignored their request. At 9:15 on the morning of August 6th, a single American B-29, a Boeing Superfortress bomber, the famous *Enola Gay*, piloted by Colonel Paul Tibbets, dropped the atomic bomb it carried, called "Little Boy," over Hiroshima. The explosion instantly killed some 70,000 people and injured another 70,000 Japanese citizens as they began their day's chores. Many more were to suffer painful deaths from radiation sickness and burns in the days and years to follow. Approximately 60% of Hiroshima was destroyed by this single bomb.

Winston Churchill noted, "By God's mercy, British and American science outpaced all German efforts." Bohr's group had bested Heisenberg's.

Only years later would we fully learn of the extraordinary efforts needed and taken by Americans to enter this atomic age. Luckily for us, Germany had not been first to create this monster.

The news was coming fast and furious now, punctuated by an eerie concomitant quietness. Knowledgeable people were terrified by the step that had been taken in mastering one of nature's best-kept secrets: how to manipulate atoms to destroy each other and in the process release untold quantities of energy. These were heady times; the atomic bomb topic was on every Askovian's lips.

Japan's arrogant military idiots still refused to quit, so on August 9th, a few hours after Russia had declared war on Japan, another American B-29 Superfortress, named the *Great Artiste*, piloted by Major Sweeney, dropped "Fat Boy", a significantly improved version of the Hiroshima bomb, on Nagasaki. This bomb used plutonium instead of uranium as the fission material, resulting in a bigger bang. The primary target had been Kokura, but because of bad weather the major selected his secondary, Nagasaki. Again the results in death and destruction were staggering.

Incredibly, the Japanese warriors still did not want to quit, but thank God their emperor decided this was enough and declared the war over, agreeing to unconditional surrender. Finally the Japanese surrendered unconditionally to General MacArthur on the U.S. battleship *Missouri* in Tokyo Bay. The Asian nightmare had ended while giving birth to the nuclear age.

To this day there remain deep troubling concerns over the moral issues of America having resorted to using atomic forces to terminate the Asian war. At the end it was largely the innocent civilian populations of two Japanese cities that paid the price for their warlord's stubbornness.

Why can we not learn that war is hell?

Those of us who were a scant couple of years from being drafted felt a very strong sense of relief. Simultaneously we sensed we were stepping into a frightening new period of history, as now the stage had been forever set for possible world annihilation. This foreboding cloud could only be respected, never toyed with. How was this genie to be controlled?

Nineteen forty-five had been a busy year for America. We'd seen the death of President Roosevelt, sobering victory on two continents, the beginning of a new age, international trials, and so on. After the war, America rightfully celebrated its new status as the world's most powerful conquering nation. Less rightfully, Americans began to gloat. But of course we were not the only powerful nation on earth. We had a ruthless competitor, the USSR, a nation that at that time was equally vile as the two nations we had just defeated.

For the moment the shooting wars were over, but the cold war was rapidly filling the void. Real peace would remain tenuous for years to come.

Perhaps the paramount outcome of the previous five years was that America now began to assume the role of "Policeman to the World." We also began helping our former enemies regain productivity and a sense of dignity, unlike post-World War I.

In particular the immigrants in America eagerly supported programs to help families in their former homelands. Rebuilding the world that had gone astray became a huge task, but one that Americans assumed eagerly and with generosity.

Those who lived through this era and were at least semiconscious could not help but feel that something very profound had taken place. The world had not evolved slowly and methodically, as from an agrarian age into an industrial age. This tampering with the atomic structure had been a quantum leap for the human race. Many expressed fearful opinions to the effect that we should not be playing God. The atomic Pandora's box had been opened, never to be closed again. Humankind had achieved an incredible insight into the workings of the universe.

Are we worthy of the secret?

Just a short nine years later, I was to learn how to assemble both atomic and hydrogen bombs as an officer in the U.S. Air Force. I had been around to experience the birth of the atomic age and would soon be an active participant in preparing for the possible nuclear destruction of the planet. This experience made me feel absolutely giddy with dread, awe, and wonder.

Sadly, half a century later there is seemingly an incredible worldwide lethargy about the danger of the stockpiles of unused nuclear weapons, some of which may be up for sale to whomever has the bucks. Vigilance is difficult to sustain over any period of time. Complacency is easily acquired.

In just a decade our family had experienced a locust-infested dust bowl; a heavily rock-ridden piece of ex-tundra called Askov; a war of unbelievable brutality; and the opening of the atomic age. Ja, for sure, things were moving right along, and we still had not seen a television set or a computer.

Lessons Learned:

Nature revealed an awesome secret.

This secret is exciting—but terrifying!

Chapter 14
Grand View College

Graduation from H.C. Andersen School in June 1947 was completely anticlimactic. The wars had abated, and routine dreariness seemed to have set in everywhere. The immigrants in Askov were busily trying to send relief packages to aid the folks back home. Everyone supported the Marshall Plan; the ever-generous Americans were at it again.

In spite of the Japanese warlords' atrocities, many expressed concern, even guilt, about America having used the atomic bomb. Now the challenge was to help Asians get back to normalcy. General McArthur was making huge American-style reforms in Japan. Again, the willingness to share that characterized American immigrants was evident as Americans sacrificed to help rebuild the nations they had destroyed in their self-defense.

I vividly recall our science teacher, Mr. Trestrail, who, although down to one lung and still smoking heavily, constantly told us about atomic energy and how the world was now forever changed and the opportunities that lay ahead for humankind. Though his personal future was bleak, he exuded optimism.

Our high school years had been consumed by wars, military discussions, and the dawning of a new science—few dances or parties. There were now about a dozen of us ragtag rutabaga farm and city kids champing at the bit to move on, but to where, we for damn sure didn't know. To cap this gala graduation event, it fell to me to give a soupy "how thankful and happy we are" speech and play a cornet solo called "Liebestraum". If you know that rather dreary melody, you know it sounds exactly like a funeral dirge gone stuck. Tooting it on a cheap, tinny cornet made it sound dreadful, but high school was finally over.

Just before the ceremony my parents gave me my first wristwatch, a beautiful gold looking Elgin. I can only imagine how they had sacrificed to pay for it, but it is truly a prized possession, and I still cherish it for what it represented: a safe and secure childhood filled with love and support.

Following the grandiose graduation ceremony, we all went to our respective homes and entertained what few friends and relatives popped in for free refreshments; a sharp contrast to the expensive events and fancy clothes showered upon today's graduates.

As I was getting ready to join my colleagues in town for a modest school celebration, father came into my room and quietly thanked me for being their son and not having gotten killed or caused too much embarrassment for the family.

I shuffled my feet nervously and tried to respond that I, too, was thankful to have survived thus far. Though unspoken I instinctively knew that this was the discussion that would boost this teenage turkey out of the nest. From now on, it was clearly up to me to take care of myself and be responsible for my own future.

Free lunches were over.

Although not yet eighteen I remember this little session with my father as both a sobering awakening to reality, and the naïve, but exhilarated, realization that now I could do what I damned well pleased without parental approval. I just had to pay the way!

I recall this encounter as one of the few when my father's immigrant spirit came through loud and clear, although softly spoken. This brief moment was his way of passing on the experience he had lived through as he left his Bornholm home forever to begin a new life in America. My experience was nothing compared to his, but it was nonetheless a clean break.

It was expected of me that I would earn money for the upcoming fall college semester by working out of the home during the day, and would do chores morning and night in exchange for continuing to live at home. Just as my immigrant parents had had to cut bait when they left the old country, they were now assisting me in cutting loose from their clutches.

I have often wondered about the fact that today future generations never really do have a clean departure from their childhood. Most never go through a transition that gives them the freedom that our parents gave us. I think this is a significant problem for subsequent generation Americans.

A case can be made that it is a very selfish parental indulgence to hang on to one's progeny, which many of us are guilty of doing. As parents, too many of us live our unfulfilled aspirations through our kids. It is one thing to be proud of them; it is another to possess them. It seems that, in spite of kids being street smart, able use a dirty vocabulary, participate in risky behavior, and the like, many kids are simply not capable of charting a personal course of their own through life's tempestuous seas. Could part of the problem be that we did not give them their right to their independence at an early enough age?

There have been some interesting findings in Scandinavia to the effect that kids put into boarding schools/homes at about the high school age do much better later on in college and society. An unexpected finding in these studies uncovered the fact that their parents had fewer divorces as well. That should say something!

Grand View College in Des Moines, Iowa dates back to roughly 1886. GVC was founded to provide basic education for mainly Danish immigrants as well as some preacher training for the Danish American Evangelical Lutheran Church. Though Americanized, it was modeled after the folk high school movement in Denmark. Danish folk schools were rather like halfway houses to ease young people from the farm into the workplace. Students had to work to support themselves and were provided with instruction and discussions with working adults, many of who were practicing professionals. As a rule there were no formal grades or transcripts. This was a mellow time in higher education designed to inspire and support young people in a new land.

The concept of the folk high school should probably be revisited today in light of the general discontentment existing among this age group. Berea College in Kentucky is one of the few institutions of higher learning that does incorporate some work experiences in their program.

I made the trip from Askov to Grand View College in the fall of 1947 in my parents' Model A Ford. It was a very long drive, about two hundred miles, some on dirt roads; interstates were still a long way in the future. Since my possessions were meager, it was an easy pack and an easy unpack to my assigned room. Then the folks drove off on their way back to Askov, and my college experiences, which were to last many years, began.

My first Saturday in Des Moines, I was off to the airport to see what was flying. I had great luck in meeting a Mr. Ralph Redick, who had been a WW II pilot and later flight instructor and was now training vets to fly under the GI Bill. Unabashedly I asked Mr. Redick if they had an entry-level job.

"Sure kid," he replied. "We have lots of jobs, but we can't afford to pay you."

Darn! But I quickly recovered and suggested that maybe they could give me flying lessons instead of cash.

"Okay, why not give it a try?" said Mr. Redick, as I leaped off the floor. "You do the shit work for one day, and I'll give you one hour of flying time."

This was almost too much for a former rutabaga hoe-er. "When do I start?" I yelped, trying not to show too much enthusiasm—although I was ready to drop out of college on the spot and go flying.

"Slow down, kid," said Mr. Redick. "We can only afford to have you earn an hour and a half of flying time per week."

It took a minimum of forty hours of training to get a license, which I quickly calculated meant around thirty weeks of shit work. It for sure seemed like a long time, but it would be worth it.

I began right there and then washing windshields, vacuuming, wiping oil drippings, scrubbing toilets, sweeping floors, all in close proximity to airplanes. Just the fun of crawling in and out of a wide variety of planes in order to clean the windows and vacuum the cockpits was a big treat. One day the governor of Michigan flew in, and I got to clean his plane—wow. Life was getting good; but not at school.

GVC was noted for merriment. Communal singing was widely practiced and the college's choral groups were highly respected. Having been founded by the Dancing Danes, folk dancing was the expected norm. Anatomically and mentally I could not, and still cannot, folk dance, or any other dance, and thus was immediately seen by colleagues as a throwback to a more primitive life form. Nonetheless, I had to attend, because it was cheap and because my Uncle Joe, Dr. Johannes Knudsen, was its president.

Dr. Knudsen was an incredible person, but like all college presidents, not always well understood by the student body. He was very ebullient, well read, and had all the necessary degrees, including a Ph.D. in history. Not too well known was his deep interested in the sciences, having had early personal experiences at the University of Copenhagen with many of the scientists who were creating the atomic age in the 1930s.

GVC was proud of its Danish heritage, especially of the influence of the nineteenth-century Danish philosopher N. F. S. Grundtvig, the founder of the folk high school movement. His ideas were interesting, and controversial, in that he postulated that people are first and foremost animals, with all the problems that entails. Only after one's needs for food, warmth, sex, companionship, and so on, are satisfied, he asserted, are humans capable of a serious interest in philosophy and religion. Unless these basic animalistic forces are reconciled, humanity will never attain any veneer of civility. In short: Mind over matter—but only after the belly is full.

Adherence to this belief really does put a twist in governmental operational matters, and is probably one reason Denmark has a history and reputation of taking care of people's needs through a variety of social structures. Grundtvigian philosophy fit quite well with President Knudsen's personal convictions, because it allows for science to be a partner in the overall human drama. Uncle Joe was also, at least in my opinion, a very frustrated historian who constantly tried to reconcile the Lutheran Church's literal biblical understandings with the explosive revelations arising from the hard sciences. We would frequently discuss, quite heatedly at times, the impossibility the world's established religions, especially Christianity, ever seriously embracing modern science. These sessions often endured late into the evening after I had babysat their two daughters, Sonja and Lois, when Uncle Joe would have been at some event and returned home all fired up for debate. He had zero tolerance for much of what went on in the name of religions. Later in his life he became extremely active fighting racism in Chicago.

At this time many had fallen under the spell of the logical positivists and were convinced that scientific experimental replication was the only way of finding the "truth of the universe." Uncle Joe was highly logical and as energetic as an Eveready battery in his discussions on the universe; but he had a difficult time with the positivists' point of view.

Another frequent topic of discussion was the Danish philosopher Soren Kierkegaard, who was also influential in Danish thinking, but quite a grumpy guy. His writings were challenging and coldly logical. Much of his work questioned the veracity of the established thought of his day, especially Christianity.

Because GVC had a strong Danish liberal Lutheran affiliation, debates about philosophical and religious issues were always encouraged. This attitude was designed to help students develop a clearer understanding of one's "view of life." Dogma be damned!

In retrospect this was a period when the sciences were again seriously beginning to challenge established religions—just like when it was discovered the sun did not go around the earth. But instead of embracing the revelations about our universe there was a retreat by many to primitive times and notions—somehow it felt more comfortable. In this new millennium we are again witnessing a conservative resurgence trying to stem the tide of new knowledge.

GVC turned out to be a fantastic experience, one that I am forever grateful for, even though I did not really fit in with much of its traditional social life. But in 1947-49 the college was loaded with WW II veterans who did not give a hoot about clothes, status, or anything else, including folk dancing. I found I did fit right in with these guys without having had to go to war. They were experienced, hilarious, tough, and could get me into bars and buy beer.

This group of veterans who had shown up on the steps of higher education comprised the first wave of a segment of American males who had been through tough times. Even though they were honored and revered, they carried recent memories that haunted them. For the majority of these servicemen, the inane silliness of freshman college social life was just that.

Being the nephew of the GVC president, I became a valuable pawn as well as hostage for these WW II vets,

who took on the name "Stinky Miller Gang." The antics of the Stinky Miller Gang were on one hand hilari-
ously funny, but they often had a mean cutting edge
that eventually did them in and unduly hurt President
Knudsen.

To counteract the hippity-hopping folk dancers,
Stinky Millers initiated a ritual of some import to the
GVC male student body. It was called getting Danish
Blue Balls. You got it right.

The process began when word leaked out that
someone, a male, had a date. As the happy, unsuspecting student was getting cleaned up for the event, the
Gang would grab him and douse his private parts with
an ink, called Quink. Solemn words were spoken about
how the anointed one could now proudly go forth with
Danish Viking Blue Balls.

These were emotionally turbulent times for the service men who had been trained to kill or be killed and
now had to forget and move on to traditional academia.
Trying to recapture these lost years by resorting to rather
inane activities was at best pathetic.

The Stinky Miller antics were symptoms of frustrations; their actions seemed to suggest that they were
somehow trying to recapture youthful times lost in serving America. Many older and/or returning university
students can relate to this feeling, whether their college
experience was delayed due to military duty, the necessity to get a job, or early parenting. You do not get those
frivolous teen years back.

A major difference between the WW II and today's
vets was the drug issue. Whereas alcohol had been the
primary libation in the forty's today's servicemen have
available a plethora of mind altering chemicals.

Although Uncle Joe perceived these men as incorrigible, he never gave up hope in trying to rebuild their psyches. Sadly they were forever altered, and no matter how hard the GVC administration and faculty tried, they managed only marginal success. In my shaky role as negotiator, I quickly learned what to tell each side and what not to tell. Life as a double agent was tricky and unrewarding, so I eventually gave it up.

Looking back at this period, I do not wonder that there were problems, when so many young men had gone to war, engaged in and witnessed unspeakable slaughter, and then suddenly were expected to adjust to civilian life as college freshman. The entire GVC folk dancing bit that worked so well for teenagers did not positively attract these guys' attention. It irritated the hell out of them.

Joining their ranks in the bars late at night and listening to their war stories as alcohol softly numbed their senses was fascinating. Each session always began on a high note of dirty jokes and raucous levity, but inevitably ended in quiet sadness, often singing or wailing, "On the tables down at Morley's..." one of their favorites. They surely convinced me that anything connected to war was sheer hell. My dreams of being a fighter pilot were rapidly cooling down. The glorious war movies of the times took on a new perspective when those that had been there told "the rest of the story".

GVC was at this time fortunate to have leaders who understood and were sympathetic to a very different kind of student body. Among them was Harry Jensen who served the campus in a variety of leadership positions, and perhaps most importantly was Knudsen's personal confidant.

As a high school graduate who had not been properly prepared for college, my GVC freshman year was challenging. I had enthusiastically registered for advanced courses, even when I had never had beginning algebra or geometry. Physics, chemistry, English, and German rounded out the list. While struggling academically my mind was sitting on the runway at the airport, wishing to be in the skies above Des Moines.

I got a break in chemistry class, when the professor, Carl Strandskov, who loved his grapes, needed someone to mix reagents for the labs. It was a great job—having no schedule, good pay, and the run of the lab after hours provided some side benefits, not to be elaborated on.

Like all students, I looked forward to weekends, but not to the sporting events or folk dances. No, weekends were periods of time to devote to the captivating business of flying. A full day of work on Saturday was followed by one hour of flying on Sunday mornings. Terrific deal.

In post-WW II times, getting even a private plane license involved many of the same training exercises that had been required of wartime pilots, especially since many former military instructors were now doing civilian training. This meant we had to do lots of spins, every kind of stall imaginable, slip and slide to land fast and short—but no loops.

One day, however, Mr. Redick made a special effort to ensure I knew how to get out of the Aeronca 7AC, known as the Champ, and also that I remembered how to use the parachute. At first this did not seem significant, but shortly after we took off, Mr. Redick said we were going do to a loop.

"You must promise that you will never ever do this by yourself," he admonished.

"Yes sir."

Loops were not required for a private license and were considered risky, since should these light planes stall at the top of the inside loop, the wings would be subjected to more stress than they were designed for. As long as the plane is flying fast enough, however, there is no danger.

To loop a small plane, you begin by first diving and then pulling back on the stick and gunning the engine. This created a weird sensation. As the plane is momentarily pointed straight upward, you lose the horizon before beginning to fall back to earth. Then the horizon reappears, but from an unfamiliar and disorienting perspective. I had a great experience, and there were many times I was tempted to do one on my one, but I never did.

As the time to solo approached, after roughly eight hours of instruction, I was getting excited. One crisp cool Saturday morning, we had been out spinning and practicing touch-and-go landings, when Mr. Redick asked me to pull off the active runway and stop on the taxiway. I did, not knowing what was up. He threw open the door, got out, patted me on the shoulder, and said the plane would be a lot more responsive with his 180 pounds gone from the back seat.

"Go have fun." Wow-ee, this was to be my first solo flight! He said he would watch me do one touch-and-go landing, and if he was gone when I came around again I had passed and should go fly by myself for a couple of hours.

This was it! Taxiing back to the runway, I did notice the plane seemed to have more spunk. When the tower gave permission to take off, I could not believe how fast that little sucker could move. I was airborne in a few seconds and eagerly anticipated making my first solo landing. I came around to land, only to discover Mr. Redick already walking back to the hangar. He wasn't even going to stay and watch me—good. Being light, the little plane simply did not want to sit down, and we kept floating along, five feet above the ground. I finally had to stall hard by lifting the nose more than usual in order to land. I touched down as required and promptly began accelerating to again take off. This time I was not coming back for a while.

I left the airport airspace and headed out over the frozen Iowa farmlands, exuberant. Free to fly wherever! Time passed without my paying much attention, and all too soon the gas gauge indicated it was time to return. This time the landing went better. I taxied in, tied the plane down, and headed into the "flight room". There sits Mr. Redick, drinking his morning coffee and reading the *Des Moines Register*.

He looked over the paper, smiled and nonchalantly asked, "How did it go?"

I had no words other than, "Okay, thank you."

"Well then, you are now free to fly by yourself as long as you can afford it," he commented. He signed my logbook, which gave me permission to fly by myself. This was a lot of freedom for a teenager.

But economics ruled. While flying was awesome, I found soda fountain work tiring, experimenting freely in the chemistry lab exciting at times, college studies horribly time consuming, and money desperately short. So after getting the license, I started charging fellow students for rides. It worked.

The first year at GVC had indeed passed in a hurry. My real sense of accomplishment for that year, other than finishing the freshman courses, was having received the "single engine land" pilot's license, with no expiration date. It is still valid, half a century later—hot digiddy!

The second year at GVC went smoothly. I had acclimated to college the first year, and with subsequent success, books and academic pursuits became attractive and rewarding. Flying was now for fun, and studies were for real. Since GVC was at that time only a two-year college, my future education would be at the University of Minnesota.

Lessons Learned:

Flying was lots more exciting than studying.

Grand View College provided an excellent beginning for future studies and life style.

There's a lot to be said for Grundtvig.

We should carefully listen to our veterans.

Chapter 15
University of
Minnesota

As a student there is an enormous difference between a small, basically religious-oriented college and a major mid-western land grant university. Both have their strengths and weaknesses. Deciding which is a better choice is no easy chore, but those who never attend a large university are missing some significant experiences.

Grand View College, founded by immigrants, was a great place for a boundary layer person to come in touch, as an independent adult, with the Danish movement to America. GVC's philosophy was a tolerant mixture of the old Denmark blended into the evolving America. Students enjoyed a strong feeling of tradition, belonging, comfort, and security. In many ways it functioned as an extended family. A lot of Danish was spoken, even taught to those interested. Foods reflected the recipes brought over by our parents and grandparents. (But seldom were rutabagas served!)

Grand View College was the glorious Vikings, the

indomitable Northern warriors of the past; the University of Minnesota the golden gophers, my childhood nemeses in the rutabaga field of Askov.

To survive at a large university, then and today, students must be self-starters, be willing to ferret out information, be impervious to bureaucracy, be able to select the courses deemed important to your career, and most importantly find ways to get the right professors. Your academic future becomes your decision—very much like being an immigrant.

Ever since America's founding education had been a major concern. At the college level it was Justin S. Morrill, a United States representative and senator, who was responsible for the Morrill Acts (1862, 1890) that provided for the establishment of the "land grant" colleges. Many of these colleges quickly grew to become America's premier universities. It was my luck to become a fortunate recipient of the Homestead and Morrill Acts both designed to improve America by helping the immigrants.

Ja, for sure, I found it exciting attending the University of Minnesota, one of the largest institutions in the United States at that time. The U of M encouraged, even demanded, openness of expression in the liberal arts courses, including colorful language, fearless challenges to the instructors' lectures, and tolerance of some truly wacky ideas. Having to leave the classroom because another class was scheduled was often disappointing. Debates would be continued outside, where the professors eagerly became even more dramatic—or, in some cases, excessively melodramatic.

A well-known philosopher professor came to class one day with his fly wide open. Everyone listened dutifully while he ranted and raved about some Hindu ideas in the *Bhagavad Gita.* We all kept looking at the ceiling or sidewalls; no one dared look at another person for fear of bursting out laughing. Well, the next day this intellectual titan came to class with a huge diaper pin fastened outside of his fly. "Ha, ha! You thought I didn't notice that my fly was open, didn't you?" The class roared, and it was on to more Eastern Indian philosophy.

The science and technology courses at the U of M were noted for rigor. Naturally, enthusiasm for courses on nuclear physics was running high at this time, overshadowing many of the other sciences. Splitting the atom was viewed as potentially humankind's salvation—energy-wise. Logical positivism was the reigning, as well as raging, philosophy of the day: If you can't prove something with replicable experimentation, don't even waste your time, because it doesn't exist.

This was an exuberant period when technology was beginning to rise to the fore. Everything was considered doable. Norbert Wiener, the visionary from MIT, coined the word *cybernetics* from the Greeks, and was predicting many of the whiz-bang computer features we now take for granted fifty years later. New elements for the periodic chart were being discovered seemingly on a daily basis. The notion of creating a hydrogen bomb, earlier viewed as absurd, was now seriously envisioned as a development that would raise the ante in the conflict between America and Russia.

Many of the university professors were immigrants who had somehow escaped the tyranny of Europe prior to WW II. Quite often it was difficult to understand their lectures because of language problems, but for sure their enthusiasm and inspiration made for vibrant classes.

"What in hell was the professor talking about?" was a constant gripe. After many classes the race was on to the library to see what English books were available on the topics under discussion. Thank god the syllabi were in English.

The good professors taught, while the great professors also inspired.

Student jobs around campus, as well as dormitory housing, were plentiful. Seemingly no one slept—the university ran nonstop, with many labs all night. Research had caught on, and students were needed to watch things cook and bubble around the clock.

Students spent nights studying in the dimly lit library, catching up on lab experiments, or participating in small group discussions in dormitories or rooming houses. Weekends focused on jobs, occasionally sporting events, and sometimes a concert by the Minneapolis Symphony.

The intellectual and cultural climate throughout America was ebullient. Winning the Second World War had energized the nation. Its former soldiers, GI bill in hand, were eager to study and begin rebuilding their disrupted lives. The instrumentation developed during the war was now rapidly being applied to industry and agriculture. Just as had been the case at Grand View College, many of the newly graduated high school kids at the university did not mesh well with these highly motivated veterans. They were immature, silly, and inane by comparison. Thus, the universities of the day served a bimodal student body.

The universities of this era espoused freedom and power. The academicians were absolute monarchs, some with considerable puffery and others with touching humility. But it was becoming clear that many issues surrounding a university's operation would soon have to be faced and hopefully resolved. Most of these issues are as pertinent today as they were in the late 1940s. Let us look at a few cases.

• The struggle for **intellectual property right of ownership** was beginning to come into focus. At issue was, who should really own newly discovered scientific secrets at a state supported university? Was it the creative student who diligently collected data and saw a relationship? The guiding professor who initially structured the research? The university that provided the opportunity for experimentation? Or was it society at large, since they were paying for the entire circus? Each entity in its own way had made a significant contribution to the unveiling of a new idea. A contest over ownership was forming.

Ideas do spring from individuals, but do they not belong to all of us? No human is an intellectual island.

As Newton humbly proclaimed, "If I have seen a little further than others, it is because I have stood on the shoulders of giants."

• The desire by some universities to make **money from their athletes' performances** in order to develop magnificent sports complexes that can then make more money should be challenged. Is it the task of a university to be a sports farm for the professional teams? Sure as hell seems to be the way it is going at many universities.

- **Admissions and graduation standards**, which seemed rather benign and straightforward in the late forties, are today rightfully under attack. Do standardized admissions tests provide a fair reflection of students' accomplishments? As for graduation standards, are professors' tests biased? Of course they are, and probably should be, providing the content of the test is fairly related to the syllabus of the course.

This list of concerns expands endlessly as universities try to define themselves, their missions, and to accommodate the wide variety of students seeking admission.

This diversity of today's university students is to a large extent the result of immigrants and the eagerness of their kids to "go to the U." This variety must not be lost to some arbitrary set of conforming standards.

Foreign students now attending our colleges and universities bring an additional incredibly rich assortment of ideas and perspectives. As they learn our democratic ways and take them back to their native countries, the world becomes a slightly better place to live. Attempts to curtail this international influence are deplorable.

Everyone who lives and works in an academic environment is constantly engaged in an avalanche of issues whose solutions have far-ranging implications. In particular, the scientific findings emanating from universities, spanning astronomy to genetics to physics to zoology, now more than ever challenge our culture at large with options that require moral, ethical, political, and economic decisions. This is not only exciting stuff—

it is essential for our survival.

Fast forward – 2003: Some troubling issues are now plaguing our large, state-supported universities. Openness of expression is often curtailed for fear of being politically incorrect. This correctness malarkey is about to become detrimental to our intellectual growth and development. Discouraging or censoring open expression at the university level simply bottles up troublesome ideas, only to see them emerge later in a more virulent format. But much worse, great ideas may be squashed before they get a fair airing. America's First Amendment needs constant support.

I experienced another lucky strike while shaving one morning in Pioneer Hall, when I met a Swedish immigrant by the name of Chell Bosson, a former Olympic runner. He had purchased a tired WW II Piper Cub trainer, but he did not have a license and did not know how to fly. He had a plane, I had a license—what a match!

He kept his war surplus plane at the U of M airport north of Minneapolis, and I had a Model A that we used for ground transportation. We flew the hell out of that old plane and had a lot of fun. Eventually Chell managed to pay a real instructor and officially soloed. But he did not want to pay for additional lessons to acquire a license, making my presence essential.

Chell's nature was somewhat different from mine. He was majoring in aeronautical engineering and loathed ROTC. We were all selling blood in those days to make a couple of bucks. Chell would take his funds, buy a bottle of rum, pour himself a glassful, no ice, and sit down to read math textbooks like they were fairy tales. He was also recklessly fearless. Theoretically Chell fully understood the structural integrity of small planes, but that did not necessarily translate into safe flying procedures. At his insistence (it was his plane) we would fly under telephone and power lines—a really stupid stunt, and we're damn lucky to have lived to tell about it. You can only do these things while you are in the immortal stage of life: under twenty-one.

One cold spring weekend we decided to fly to Lake of the Ozarks to warm up a bit. At less than a hundred miles an hour, it took us many hours to get there. We landed on an ice-covered grassy field, walked into town, and had something to eat. Chell suggested we see about staying in the city jail to save some money. Sure enough, the local redneck chief of police locked us up overnight for free.

Air fairs were regular events at the U of M airport. The challenge was to fly around dropping sacks of rocks and see who could come closest to the target. To do this you needed someone to sit in the back seat to drop the sacks.

One time, I got a nervous, but eager to fly, student to be my bombardier. It was a cold winter day, as always in Minnesota, with salt spread on the tarmac to thaw the ice. We began racing down the runway, and suddenly the left wheel froze and stopped turning. We had enough speed, so with a little aileron pressure, I managed to raise the left wing and get the plane running on its right wheel. You guessed it—the right wheel froze.

The plane promptly veered into the snow bank on the right side of the runway. The kid in the back was screaming, the damn oil gauge was coming right at my forehead until the shoulder straps restrained me, and all the while the propeller is breaking into a thousand splinters.

We came to a halt with the plane stuck, nose into the snow bank, almost upside down. The prop was busted, the right wing was twisted, and the wheels were now somehow spinning. My erstwhile bombardier was coming unglued, and I was trying to figure out how in the world to pay for this mess. I was already on the ragged edge of financial insolvency.

Soon the entire observation and kibitzing gang arrived at the scene of the disaster. *What happened, what happened? Are you all okay?* My bombardier sounded as if we had just returned from a devastating fire raid over Dresden and been hit by flack and a squadron of Messerschmitts. I felt terrible, especially now that the wheels were spinning freely. But they *were* frozen.

The owner of the plane, a farm student from Montana, actually owned three planes that he used in his farm-dusting business. The only reason I had ones of his planes is that I had told him I was born in Plentywood. I guess he felt I had suffered enough, so he loaned me one of his planes.

I stuttered something to the effect that I would pay for the damage if he would just shut up my bombardier. He laughed, then said that these Piper crates were held together by wire and spit, and that if I could get him a propeller, all was forgiven. Wow!

"But there is a catch," he said. "You must take one of my other planes and do the "bomb run" all by yourself."

"No, siree," I answered, shaken up and not eager to try that again.

"If you don't do it now, I can guarantee that you will never want to fly again," he replied with some authority.

Oh, boy—I had to do it. I did, and I have never been afraid of flying since. What became of my scared bombardier? I do not know—never saw him again.

As America was spinning its way into the 1950s, troubling international issues were again arising from a variety of sources. America's relationship with the USSR continued to deteriorate. Communism was being exposed for its ruthless treatment of dissidents. Stalin may have killed more than Hitler. The cold war was beginning to heat up.

The hysterical anti-communism furor stirred up by Senator McCarthy was having a chilling effect throughout the university community. Americans were tired of war and unfortunately not paying proper attention to what was brewing in northern Asia. We all wanted to get on with our personal business and objectives.

The real eye opener came on July 3, 1950, as the North Korean armies began moving southward after crossing the 38th parallel. They quickly reached Seoul, South Korea's capitol. America had again been caught unprepared for what was to come, namely an undeclared war that went by the name of police action and would eventually cost America 50,000 casualties, not to mention the wounded and economic losses. The other unfortunate participants suffered equal or worse losses, especially Korea, both North and South.

My final days at the U of M were becoming similar to my final days of high school. War was again on the horizon, coming ever closer, and the atomic bomb was readily available.

I found getting part-time jobs while a student at the U of M to be quite easy and lucrative. Good luck

had gotten me into the Pioneer Hall kitchen floor mop-
ping business, and that parlayed into a summer camp
job at Camp Lincoln for Boys, located on Lake Hubert
in central Minnesota. This was a camp for the sons of
the rich and famous. Here I met Ruth.

Ruth was a very athletic and outgoing girl, having
played varsity basketball in Des Moines, Iowa. I met
her in the kitchen where we both worked doing dishes
and general grunt duties. As kitchen workers we had a
great time, which translated into supplying the camp
kids—whose parents were paying megabucks for this
experience—with contraband ice cream, cookies, late-
night canoe rides, and other off the record activities.

Two unexplainable experiences were to occur. At
the end of the summer, Ruth left for a college she was
attending in Chicago, and I returned to the U of M. The
fun-filled summer camp experience had turned to
memories.

In mid-November I was working with a buddy in
the laundry at the U of M hospital, hanging wet sheets
on a stick to later be fed into mangles. Suddenly, I had
a very strange visual experience of seeing Ruth on a
hospital gurney being wheeled down a hospital corri-
dor. It was a clear picture full of details. The guy I was
working with asked me what was wrong. Apparently I
had become still and turned ashen. I told him about
the "vision". We both dismissed the episode as the result of too-long working hours and bad hospital food,
and went about our business; but I could not get over
it.

Upon returning to my rooming house after midnight, I found a phone message from Ruth's mother
asking me to call her immediately. When I did so, she
told me that Ruth had tried to commit suicide that night

by taking carbolic acid at the end of a streetcar line in Des Moines. Wow.

As I slowly got over the shock and was told that Ruth had been taken to the hospital and was recovering, I had to ask. "When did this happen?"

Her answer shook the bejesus out of me. It was exactly at the time, as best I could determine, when I had had the vision of Ruth lying on a hospital gurney.

Not being experienced in this sort of thing, I had to get some answers. I drove to Des Moines and talked with Ruth and family members. The trip yielded no clues from anybody, except that the timing of the event and vision were to the minute. My Uncle Joe had no explanation, but said he would talk to some medical friends.

Time went on, and I thought less and less of the event. However, a few months later, I was on my way to class on a cold, frosty Minnesota morning, thinking about an upcoming math exam. As I trudged across a snow-covered parking lot, I felt an incredible wave of elation. I had never felt so good. It only lasted a few seconds, but . . . For a second time in three months I had been strangely jolted by something I could not explain. I did not make a connection to the earlier vision. There had been no vision this time, just a fantastic joyous feeling.

Onward I went to the test, then to the library, and later that day back to the rooming house—where I found another phone message to call Ruth's mother immediately. *Now what?*

Ruth had finally found the peace she was seeking, I was told. Her suicide attempt that morning, by hanging in their garage, had been successful. *Oh, no!* Would I come to the funeral? *Of course.* My Uncle Joe and his wife Aunt Ellen went with me. I told Uncle Joe I had to know what time of day Ruth was pronounced dead. He said he would find out.

Yes, it was, as best as could be determined by the coroner, exactly the time I had experienced the feeling of elation as I walked through the snow. I had absolutely no explanation for these two events. In my mind, however, I was willing to entertain the notion that there may indeed be other dimensions to this universe that we have yet to understand.

Knowing someone who suddenly takes his or her life was a shock. Suicide is the sort of thing you read about, but unless you are close to it, it is only a conversation topic. But when it is someone you know, you become depressed and begin thinking about how it might have been prevented, which leads to remorse and guilt. On top of that, I had the unaccounted-for associated image and feeling.

There was no one I could really discuss this topic with who I felt made any sense. So I decided to take a couple of elective psychology courses. After all, the U of M faculty was supposed to be the font of all knowledge. That turned out to be a very stupid decision. The two courses I selected were in the area of abnormal psychology. I immediately discovered that most, if not all, of the students, as well as faculty, were not there dispensing knowledge; on the contrary, they were all, like me, seeking answers. Not very reassuring.

The lab assignments accompanying the classroom lectures entailed spending time in a nearby mental institution. That was really tough. This was the era when electric shock was being peddled as the hot ticket to sanity. I could never figure out how pumping millions of volts into a body that normally runs on mille-volts would provide a cure for madness. I guess when you are desperate enough you will try anything.

I did not get stellar grades in these psychology courses. But worse, I did not get any closer to understanding my eerie experiences. These courses were by far the most depressing academic experiences imaginable. For the many unfortunate deranged patients we observed, there seemed to be no cure, only uncontrolled emotions and behaviors that were destroying them and their loved ones.

I was, and continue to be highly skeptical about extrasensory experiences, but I am convinced that our understanding of phenomena like this is still limited. On the other hand, I find it strangely reassuring to have a modest conviction, based on these mysterious experiences, that perhaps there are levels of activity going on all around us that we have yet to discover.

My last year at the U had been an emotional roller coaster, and now an ominous future loomed, as warring in Korea had become a sure bet. Many of us of draftable age were debating this new Asian conflict and how should we prepare for it. The options were simple: enlist or be drafted.

By this time the U of M had hooked me on becoming a perpetual student. I found the opportunity to go to exciting and challenging classes rewarding as well as entertaining. Today, with the Internet, it is easier for people to be perpetual students. Even so, I find it sad that more people do not have access to stimulating learning environments or aspire to the business of teaching and learning as a lifelong vocation.

Too many stop learning – much too soon.

I couldn't help but notice that university professors often had a laboratory (which is really an adult sandbox) to play in and they got paid—not a bad deal at all, thought I. University teaching, as a job, was subtly beginning to have a personal appeal. The Pine City draft board had kindly delayed my military induction so I could finish my degree. In the spring of 1952 I enlisted in the United States Air Force. My wonderful experiences at the University of Minnesota had come to an end, and I was off to war—something I had so desired as a youth ten years earlier. But now I was less certain about being a warrior. Funny what a few years of aging can do to one's perspective! Luckily I was to return to the U of M many years later.

Lesson Learned:

There is no better life than at a university.

Perhaps there more dimensions to life.

Model of atomic bomb "Fat Boy".

Chapter 16
Korean Police Action

We had reached the mid-twentieth century, and a large segment of the world was again in a warring mode. The fledgling United Nations and all the other local alliances that had been established were ineffective in preventing another conflagration. Again we were asking, Why do humans continually fail to learn to live together—peacefully? The fuss was now over the 38th parallel in Korea.

University life was finished, at least for a while, and national duty was calling. While not necessarily excited about the military, I still felt a lingering instilled patriotism from the recent World War II. In addition, a nagging respect arose for the truism:

**When your dreams begin becoming regrets,
you are getting older.**

Damn, it was time to get into this war and see about flying. It would be now or never.

The Korean "police action" seesawed back and forth in the early 1950s. General MacArthur was getting under Truman's skin, until he was rather ignominiously canned in April 1951. The general's speech about how "old soldiers never die, just fade away" stirred many veterans and active duty soldiers. However, warfare as it had been practiced was changing. The Korean conflict became a harbinger of the kinds of wars that were to follow. The public expressed concern and fear over the possibility of another application of nuclear weaponry.

Off I went to Lackland Air Force Base in San Antonio, Texas for basic training. Being the oldest enlistee, they put me in charge of getting about thirty of us burrheads from Minneapolis to San Antonio on a half-assed troop train. By the time the train got to Bloomington, on the outskirts of Minneapolis, a ride of five miles, everyone except me was roaring drunk and stayed that way to San Antonio.

As we passed through the then dry state of Oklahoma, I was instructed by the train folks to see that no more alcohol was consumed. Right! We did have one hell of a two-day train party, and I did get all of us, albeit of somewhat uneasy gait, to Lackland AFB. After proudly presenting our enlistment papers to a sergeant, I was severely dressed down for the condition of my charges.

The fact that I had not volunteered for this job was a useless plea. As a matter of fact, this weak alibi was viewed as insubordination, and I was assigned demerits to work off—before training had even begun. The more I thought about this event, the more depressed I became, in that I had stayed sober the entire time thinking I was doing my patriotic duty. A new thinking paradigm was obviously needed if one was to cope with military minds.

Basic training during wartime was a rugged experience. Hazing and every demeaning activity the trainer morons, loosely called drill sergeants, could conceive of were not only allowed, but encouraged. You learned to survive hour by hour. We learned that there are more than twenty-four hours in a day.

This intensive training was viewed as preparation in the event we should ever be taken prisoner in North Korea. World War II was still very much in the military's mind, and they knew only too well how the Japanese and Germans had treated American prisoners. The training program did have a purpose; the problem was that we trainees just didn't like it.

Miserable as the drill instructors made this experience, there was a certain benign challenge to beat them at their own game. We began forming alliances with anybody and everybody who was not one of them. We really did learn to depend on each other for everything, especially keeping our mouths shut or how to lie if that served the cause better. The grand basic training strategy works:

Cooperate to graduate.

We had in our squadron a former Minnesota pig farmer lad by the name of Porath—not Askovian, but could have been—who had never been washed since his mother delivered him. He was a stinking embarrassment, not to mention being superbly proud of his condition, an attitude bordering on in-your-face arrogance. We were pressured by our masters (drill sergeants) to do something about Airman Porath's aroma, or we would all participate in lots of undesirable activities.

What to do, and still stay within bounds? Late one evening after taps, we spread-eagled stinky Porath on the cold tiled shower floor and scrubbed the bejesus out of him with brooms and lye soap. Like a larva after metamorphosis, Porath was now the cleanest damn airman in the US Air Force. That night he learned a lesson in keeping his body from smelling, and—surprise!—became a great buddy. He had just needed to have his attitude tweaked. He never held any grudges and accepted this experience with aplomb and dignity. This is for sure not a recommended, let alone sanctioned, training technique, but you just never know what will work.

Now bad luck befell me, in that I was assigned to be the right guard. Being right guard simply meant you had to march in front by yourself and set some kind of cadence for the rest to follow. Thus, any and everything that went wrong behind you was naturally your screw-up. This scapegoat assignment is usually reserved for short guys, so I qualified. During formal dress parades it was the most uncomfortable position; all too often I had the mischievous desire to lead the entire half-asleep bunch right off the parade field back into the mess hall.

Finally the day came when we had successfully completed months of basic training and awaited our new assignments. Here comes good ole Porath, big smile, squeaky clean, trying to collect a cash "gift" to express gratitude to our wonderful barbaric drill sergeant for making us killer soldiers.

This caper caught most of us the wrong way. It was absolutely illegal, and I suspected that Porath had been set up by our criminally insane drill sergeant. I protested, refused to go along with the shakedown, and suggested the others resist this kind of extortion. What did we have to lose? Basic training was finished, and we were about to leave. Boy, was that stupid thinking. Soon our flight was called upon by our non-benevolent drill sergeant to ostensibly perform an essential chore some distance from the barracks. We marched to the site, but no mission seemed to materialize. After a period of time, we marched back. I was now to discover that all my clothes and personal belongings, including suitcase, had disappeared into thin air. The devious sergeant gleefully informed me that I could not leave and was threatened with having to repeat basic training if I did not get a complete set of military clothes before our scheduled departure later that night.

As those of you who have been in the service all know, the military gives you your first set of duds, but the next ones you have to buy yourself at the Base Exchange with your own meager earnings. There went all the money I had saved over several months for my leave. The U.S. military teaches many different kinds of lessons.

It was off to Denver, Colorado for first-job training school, which taught how to make career assignments and read job descriptions. This was dull as hell, requiring typing and filing forms in quadruplicate day after day. No copy machines yet—carbon paper proliferated, causing purple-stained fingers and uniforms. This was indeed a long, long way from zipping around the skies in a fighter plane.

While in Denver I met Eleanor Jungck, a student nurse at a local hospital. She came from a large German family whose farm was in Rushville, Nebraska.

Rushville was a typical western grain farming community with a work force composed primarily of Native Americans. Among them there was plenty of poverty and alcoholism.

After I'd known Eleanor for only a short period of time, we decided to get married at her home the following December. In the six months until then, we would each continue with what we were doing.

My first duty assignment was to Donaldson Air Force Base in Greenville, South Carolina and a premier lesson in racism and bigotry. Getting off the train early in the morning, I found a bus going to the base and asked the driver to wake me if I fell asleep. Being the only rider, I went to the back seat, stretched out, and promptly drifted off. I soon awakened to observe six black males standing at the back, while I was the only one seated.

"Why are you guys standing?" I asked in sleepy befuddlement.

In silence, one of them pointed to a sign at the front of the bus, which said, "Whites seat from front, Negroes from rear." *What the hell?* The implications caught me completely off guard.

Gaining composure, I finally asked incredulously, "If I move to the front of the bus, will you guys sit down?"

The man nodded, I moved to the front, and we all sat down. Oh, boy, did I have a lot to learn about the Deep South, which I did over the next few months.

Prior to getting married I rented a one-room apartment above a garage in downtown Greenville. The landlady was a kindly elderly white widow who enjoyed going to a fundamental Baptist church, but had no way to get there. So I offered to take her. Shucks, she might lower the rent—but no such luck.

One day, while driving her home from her church, she was pontificating about how holy Sunday was for her, so much so that she absolutely could not do anything on that day, including writing a letter. I ask her how she justified having her black gardener come on Sunday and do all her yard work.

"Aren't you stretching this 'do no work on the Sabbath' concept a bit?" I asked.

"Oh, no," she told me. "You silly Yankees just don't understand that darkies are not quite human."

That was the last time this religious bigot got a ride to church, or anywhere else, from me. I limited our conversations to "Here is the rent" at the beginning of each month. The situation made me sad; she was otherwise a nice lady.

Back in the early fifties, the racism America had experienced until then was getting ready to explode. White people who had grown up with racist attitudes were passing them on, through both personal behavior and the formal education systems, including their religious establishments. Incredibly they never really bothered to understand what was happening until it blew up in their faces. Any half-wit could see it was coming.

For the most part the immigrants who came from Africa to America did not come voluntarily, like people of other nationalities. They came as captives. Most of the conditions that existed for other nationalities did not apply to the early black immigrants. They did not get the same sought-after freedoms they were supposedly entitled to after the Civil War, until America went through more bloodletting. Instead of freedom, America represented enslavement to them.

I felt encouraged to see that, for the most part, the U.S. Air Force encouraged blacks and whites to be seen together on the streets as long as we were in uniform; but in civvies, this practice was frowned upon by some of the locals. Open dating across bloodlines was for sure taboo.

Greenville was physically a beautiful place, but at that time it seemed to be going nowhere, and neither was I. So the idea of moving on to become an officer and maybe get to fly again came to mind. To do this, however, you had to add another four years to the basic enlistment. I took some tests, passed, and headed back to Lackland AFB for officer training.

This was more of the same demeaning treatment we had had in basic, except a whole lot rougher and more serious. Many in our flight did not finish. They carted one guy out one night in a straight jacket, kicking and screaming the entire time.

One has to admire the way the military has evolved in terms of its training practices. The degree of rigor can perhaps be debated, but the rationale for their training certainly seems to be sound. A strong case can probably be made that any governmental official having the authority to make the ultimate decision about going to war must have had some military experience, beyond the national guard. Military leaders generally do not have a taste for blood. Too often it is the politicians who have been spared from performing military service who are making these life-and-death decisions. I am forever haunted by the war experiences told to me by the GVC vets in the bars in East Des Moines.

We were administered a variety of psychological tests. I recall constantly being asked to study nondescript inkblots and then questioned about what I saw. This was a time when it was believed, with little supporting data, that these tests could somehow indicate what kind of an officer you would become.

Picture driving a large truck filled with armed soldiers down a steep hill as the brakes fail. Alas, what to do? Would you protect your mighty troops while driving over a helpless little girl crawling in a torn dress in the road, or would you risk killing the mighty troops by swerving off the unfenced road into a deep ravine, thereby sparing the child? Duh. I guess your response was then somehow used to decide what kind of an officer you would become. Big flaw in this test item—officers aren't suppose to drive trucks.

My desire, as well as the possibility, to become a fighter pilot remained. The Korean War was howling full blast, although no one seemed to know where it was going, but pilots were needed, so several of us again applied for flight training.

After an all-night cold and wet march doing military things, those of us who wanted to be pilots were taken for our flight physicals. We all flunked the vision test—couldn't even see the wall on which the eye chart hung, let alone read it. But we were told that we could reapply in a few weeks. We were never given that second opportunity.

Once the OCS training was over, military life improved markedly—better living quarters, better food, more money, and other perks. There is a huge divide between enlisted ranks and officers, even if you are only the lowest as a second lieutenant. Now the nagging question for me became: Is there flying ahead?

My first officer assignment was to Biloxi, Mississippi, at Keesler AFB. We were a relatively small class and had known each other since OCS. Keesler was an electronics school and provided superb technical education.

The theory was presented in a typical classroom setting, followed immediately by laboratory applications in a room next door. The American military is to be applauded for its incomparable ability to train people. Many years later, after become a teacher, I frequently wished our schools could apply some of the highly efficient training techniques that are so well honed by the military, especially in areas of technology. Tying theory and practice together in concentrated blocks of time produces better results more effectively, and no doubt more inexpensively. The focus of our training was radar instrumentation and wave-guides—very interesting stuff, but why? We would find out six short months later.

Lessons Learned:

America's military has done much to alleviate racism—but the task is not yet over.

Chapter 17
Nuclear Weaponry

By 1953 the Korean conflict had become a grinding, grueling campaign, inflicting heavy casualties on both sides, moving back and forth across rocky Korea with no real sense of how it was going to end. Eisenhower was the new president and had a lot of popular support. His WW II successes gave many a sense of confidence the outcome would be successful in Asia. Few had any real feeling for his sidekick Nixon; they just knew they didn't want to buy a used car from him.

The fear of getting the Chinese and Russians too deeply involved in this conflict was challenging America's leaders. There was still great uncertainty about how to work with the Asian nations. Few Americas spoke any of their languages, and fewer yet understood their longstanding customs. At this time America finally began to appreciate the value of the Asian immigrants.

The Rosenbergs were executed as atomic spies in 1953. I was jerked back nine years to the 1944 Grand View College summer camp when we were first told of the atomic device being detonated at Alamogordo, N.M. The idea that now an alien nation, Russia, was surreptitiously receiving our topmost military secrets was both maddening and frightening. Why had they sold out? With the Korean conflict in limbo, the concern over nuclear weapons hung heavily over everyone's future. The geopolitical discussions at this time included nuking Russia and China. Horrid thoughts.

Flyers were still needed in Korea, and several of us again tried to apply for flight training. We were constantly stalled on reapplying and had no choice but to continue our electronic training at Keesler AFB in Biloxi, Mississippi. Why?

The plan began to unfold when we received our first duty assignment to Kirkland AFB in Albuquerque, New Mexico. Everyone knew what New Mexico was about. The first atomic device, Trinity, had exploded here in August 1945. Los Alamos, where much of the science for the bomb had taken place, was just up the hill. Sandia Corporation, the super-secret atomic industry, was the main game all around Albuquerque.

The plan became clear. Our little bunch had probably been targeted early on for this assignment and never did have a chance of becoming flyers. The USAF needed folks to fuss with nuclear bombs, and we were to be it. I could only marvel at the strange observation that this atomic thing had seemingly followed me from tenth grade.

Upon arriving at Kirkland AFB, we were immediately up to our yoo-hoos in security paperwork. To be a nuclear weapons officer, you needed both a "Q" clearance from the civilian Atomic Energy Commission and a "Top Secret" clearance from the military. I later discovered that agents had even visited Father's family in

Bornholm, Denmark and questioned them about my character. They confided that they had said absolutely nothing, figuring I was in trouble and anything they added to my predicament would only make it worse. Good family! I did thank them years later.

Part of the mystique of this assignment was that everyone was afraid to discuss anything that remotely had to do with what we perceived was to be our lot. Daily lectures and printed material constantly stressed the need to keep your mouth shut—and it worked. The security business took several weeks; some never did get cleared and were never seen again. They probably got to fly.

Finally the clearances arrived and school began. For several days we were severely lectured about security issues and the punishment that would befall us should we fail to heed the rigorous restrictions: No sharing of any information whatsoever with family or friends. No discussing of what we learned in school among ourselves outside the classrooms. Each sheet of paper we received for keeping notes was numbered and taken from us as we left the classrooms. It was eerie to say the least, and we were all frightened.

Then came the content lectures and restricted photos of what had taken place in Hiroshima and Nagasaki, Japan, those fateful August days in 1945. There was no chitchat; instead we experienced a very queasy feeling about what this nuclear weaponry was capable of doing. After the initial flush of excitement wore off, we became a melancholy lot. As the lectures progressed everyone became deeply serious, almost morbid. Gruesome presentations, with data, of the potential for total annihilation of humankind became debilitating. The process influenced our social life. We drank sparingly, even though it was cheap, for fear that something would be said that shouldn't be.

Any person who trains for military service related to atomic, biological, or chemical warfare has my sympathy. If you have any feelings at all about humanity, receiving this kind of knowledge is overpowering and numbing. To reiterate, I find it deplorable and tragic that those politicians who are seemingly ready to go to war have not had an in-depth military experience that would provide them with a personal understanding of the magnitude and severity of these weapons.

After one class period on the physical attributes of the bombs, it was announced we would be going to the classified atomic museum to view replicas of the bombs and see more photos. When we got inside the super-secret building, no one said a single word for several hours. We were in shock as we touched and viewed prototypes of "Fat Boy" and the hardware used in making the bomb. We saw pictures of historical events in nuclear physics and of accidents that had taken place in building "the Bomb".

Our lectures consisted of technical information, along with fascinating geopolitics regarding the power structure of America, the USSR, and China. We studied secret reports, including demographics, on the potential targets that the US would nuke should it become necessary. Geography surrounding the major cities in Russia and potential targets was examined, but our instructors acknowledged that America was woefully short of reliable information.

Determining the optimum altitude to detonate a nuke in order to create the maximum destruction became a daily classroom exercise. The concern here is that if there is not enough air pressure on top of the explosion, the bomb will blow a hole in the atmosphere, allowing the energy to leak out into space, thus doing less than its optimum in destroying the target. Learning how to kill and destroy people to the max—what a (sickening) challenge.

Finally the schooling ended and we were all sent our different ways. After we parted we did not keep in touch, even though we had known each other through various training programs, beginning with OCS. Even though we had not experienced nuclear explosions, the training had changed us. The unhappy fate that befell various airmen who served on the *Enola Gay* vividly illustrates the impact that this power demon had on people.

It was on to Deep Creek Air Force Station, located behind Fairchild AFB in Spokane, Washington for three years of nuclear weapon chores. Again, with very tight security, we could not leave the base without first letting security personnel know where we were going and when we would be back. At no time could we be more than two hours away from our duty stations. This was wartime without shooting. The restrictions took their toll, since we were never really free of our obligation unless on leave, and even then they wanted to know where in hell you were at all times.

One night, when it was my turn to be OD (Officer of the Day), I had just stretched out on a cot to rest when the red phone beside the cot began to ring. The red phone was hooked up to General LeMay's Strategic Air Command Office in Nebraska, and it was only supposed to ring when a war was imminent. But here, sure as shit, it was a-ringing.

I leapt up, grabbed it, and identified myself. The code I received indicated things were indeed heating up, somewhere in Asia. After confirming with the caller the assigned codes for that day, I headed for the TWIX (teletype) machine to get a supporting printed message:

Implement the war reserve plan.

This meant to immediately begin recalling all personnel to the base, getting nuclear bombs assembled and loaded onto planes, and making other preparations to launch a nuclear strike. Within two hours all the assigned officers and airmen were in place. Two wings of B-52s, 92nd and 99th, were being loaded with atomic and hydrogen bombs, with engines running, waiting to be told to go to war. I had never been so scared in my life. Additionally we could not share this fear with anyone.

The orders were a response to the Chinese shelling of Quemoy, a small island off of Taiwan. America saw this as a provocation that had to be addressed immediately, and so we began rattling our nuclear war sabers. No one could leave the base until the alert was called off.

Historically this was a very tense period. The Chinese were for sure mad at America after the mess in Korea. Furthermore we had supported the Chinese who had left mainland China for Taiwan, and now the mainlanders were spoiling to somehow get their island back. The somewhat questionable communist link between China and Russia presented a global challenge.

After a week of this high readiness condition, the mainland Chinese stopped their provocation, and tensions cooled. The nukes were off-loaded from the planes, the "caps" (nuclear components) safely returned to AEC, and we all headed for the officer's club. Naturally we all felt a sense of relief, but tinged with the awareness that tensions in the world had not been relieved, just put on hold for another day. There was no sense of victory, just a respite. Since we were not allowed to discuss the event with anyone, including family, we became more introspective and grumpy.

My first son, Alex, was born on Fairchild Air Force Base. Being a new father added joy and a deepening sense of responsibility to my daily chores. He was and is a great kid, but I do remember the anxiety as we pondered his, and every kid's, future, given our potential for mass destruction.

The almost daily incidents on the station would make interesting history, but perhaps they are best forgotten. A somewhat funny event occurred one night as the base was doing an "exercise". These were always conducted late at night when the weather was vilely inclement. I was in charge of a base function having to do with hauling nuclear bombs around. This meant picking them up at their stored AEC igloos, hauling them to the assembly bays, and then on to the Fairchild AFB flight line, where we were also responsible for hanging them in B-36s, B-47s, or B-52s as assigned. I had about sixty guys and a fantastic Master Sergeant, Smith.

This dark, snowy, miserable early morning, around 2 AM, we were having one of these practice drills. Bombs were being toted all over the base, pulled by 6x6 trucks. Our status board was abuzz with data. As each bomb reached the final staging area, it was fully accounted for by lots of high ranking military officers and the civilian Atomic Energy Commission. Everybody had to sign everything.

Wouldn't you know it, I get a call from the base commander yelling that one of our bombs didn't show up and is now listed as lost. Not good.

"How in the hell could you lose an atomic bomb on our tiny, secure base, Lieutenant?" roared the colonel.

"Gee, sir, gosh, sir, I don't know, sir," I muttered. When you are in trouble in the service, always pepper your remarks with lots of sirs. This gives you small increments of time to think up an excuse.

"Sergeant Smith, where in the hell is one of our now-reported-missing nuclear bombs?" I feebly barked, trying to be authoritative like the colonel.

"Gosh, sir, gee, sir, I haven't a clue, sir," replied Sgt Smith.

"Well, we sure as hell better find it, or we will be civilians by morning."

"Yes, sir, I will go looking for it, sir, right now, sir." Smith jumped into our assigned small blue Air Force pick-up and sped away into the cold snowy night.

I was thinking this was not going to do my effectiveness report any good, when suddenly Sgt Smith roared in, grabbed six guys, and yelled to me he has found the goddamn bomb in a snow-covered ditch and for me to get ready to call the Base Commander.

Incredibly, Sgt. Smith and his men manually pulled the Mark 6 atomic bomb out of the ditch, hooked it up to his little pickup, towed it to the staging area, and re-connected it to its intended 6x6 truck—all without being detected, thanks to the raging snowstorm.

Then he rushed back in, shouting, "Tell the goddamn commander we don't know what he is talking about. I just saw the goddamn bomb properly attached to its assigned goddamn delivery truck."

Goddamn is used by the military for emphasis.

In a subdued, but official, tone I gingerly informed our commander that the purportedly missing bomb had just been confirmed by my first sergeant as properly attached to its tow truck. "There must be some misinformation in the field, sir."

"You'd better not be shitting me, Lieutenant! I will see both you and your first sergeant in my office when this exercise is over, you got that?"

It was a long night and morning, and when it ended Sgt. Smith and I were ushered into the base commander's office, where we were told to stand at attention.

The colonel began one royal chewing out. I was thinking that I was about to be busted back down to an Askovian rock pile rutabaga farmer, all because of one momentarily misplaced atomic bomb. Life is not fair.

When you are getting laced down in the military, you learn to mentally hunker down and wait for the tempest to blow over. Sure enough it did blow over, though his loud yelling, spiced with profanity, had now been heard by everyone in the building. He had abundantly made his point: we should definitely not lose any more atomic bombs—at least not on his base. Hard to disagree with that decision.

As quickly as the verbal storm had begun, he lowered his voice and quietly told us to be at ease and sit down. *Now what?*

Almost jovially he expressed his gratitude to us for having made the lost weapon appear as an idiotic oversight on the part of one of his immediate brown-nosing subordinates and an equally arrogant member of the AEC. I am sure he was gloating internally.

"Tonight the drinks in the club are on me," he finished. "Go get some rest. You are dismissed."

The incident was immediately over. He also re-neged on the drinks.

Finally the Korean Conflict ended in some kind of half-assed truce, which to this day still seems to be the case.

On March 1, 1954 a hydrogen fusion device was detonated on Eniwetok Atoll in the mid-Pacific with an explosive equivalency of twelve to sixteen megatons. We had entered the H-bomb era. I remember seeing my first H-bomb—it was huge. Since it required an atomic bomb for ignition, it was both a fission and a fusion evice. One of these demons is capable of com-pletely destroying any city on the planet.

We drew straws to see who would have the oppor-tunity to witness a nuclear explosion, whether in the Pacific or Western United States. I never got a winning straw, but that may have been just as well.

This Cold War era, which extended for decades, was a period that constantly challenged the existence of the human species. The number of weapons and their total destructive capacity is still not fully appreciated, un-derstood, or maybe even known. Humans now have the capability of ruining the planet with blasts and le-thal radiation that will linger eons after the explosion's noise and heat have subsided. Funny as *Dr. Strangelove* may seem, the movie is pure gallows humor.

The various accounts of people who were in some-way associated with nuclear weapons are not particu-larly uplifting. Many of us who were involved at this low operational level of nuclear weaponry were not a particularly happy bunch. Attempts at partying, en-joying outdoor and indoor events, even fishing and ski-ing were not very successful. Those of us who were privy to the atom's destructive capability and witnessed lots of reckless behavior observed that the probability of a major accident was greater than zero.

Edward Teller, the atomic physicist who is credited with fathering the abominable hydrogen bomb, was never viewed as a comic. Nuclear weaponry has got to be an inherently depressing career choice unless you are some kind of a zealot with a burning death wish. Experiences with these weapons was emotionally draining for many of us. Even without having been in combat we had scars from knowing what was now humankind's capability for global destruction. Simply put—it is distressing.

There is one tiny possible redeeming glimmer of optimism about these horrific weapons. This redemptive possibility centers on a time in the future when we discover an asteroid inbound for planet earth. At that time our only salvation may be a nuke, or bunches of them, sent hurtling into space to greet the incoming visitor and blow it asunder or alter its trajectory. The dinosaurs had no such option.

A strong case can also be made that it was for sure best that America got nuclear weaponry first and has since then been instrumental in its control, although that may now be less true than it was.

Our nation is now faced with perhaps an even greater scientific decision. This concerns the entire field of genetic engineering. If we do not assume the leadership role here, we will become the victims of this emerging science. The genie in the bottle of knowledge is loose, and trying to stuff him—(or is it a her?) —back in the bottle is a losing proposition.

It is simultaneously sad and stupid that so many believe it is possible to go back to the way things were (as they imagine it) and act as if knowledge and scientific curiosity do not exist.

Science not only exists, it prevails. Why can't we understand and appreciate what is being revealed to us?

After three years of hauling and screwing atomic bombs together in Spokane, my extended tour of duty almost over, the USAF offered me an opportunity to be assigned in Heidelberg, Germany if I would—what else—re-up for the better part of eternity?

What to do? Becoming a parent was a most exciting event, but raising my son in an atmosphere devoted to mass destruction did not sit well. I could just hear his reply in fifth grade when a colleague asks, "What does your father do?" and he has to say, "He plays with hydrogen bombs." I felt tempted to stay nonetheless, but I knew it would, in all probability, result in a lifetime military career. Inwardly I did not have the fortitude to look at these monstrously destructive devices for the rest of my life. It was time to leave and give someone else this debilitating opportunity.

However, you do not leave such experiences behind easily. Did I forget to mention that the bombs' sizes and sleek appearances are deceptive—almost beautiful? It was still, and remains, impossible for me to comprehend the awesome physical meaning of Einstein's Theories, even after years of experiences and education. The energy of the stars is truly awesome, certainly beyond the comprehension of this former Askovian rutabaga hoe-er.

From our standpoint half a century later, we see there are still rogue powers everywhere that seek to have the capability of nuclear weapons, clean or dirty. Some relatively unstable nations already have them. Any nation that may one day have nuclear capability coupled with suicidal tendencies presents a frightening scenario indeed.

As long as some people believe that the afterlife is going to be a hell of a lot better than this one, there are going to be problems here in River City.

Later I will try to make the point that we must accept the challenge to educate the entire world. It is not only our moral duty to educate the world, but it is critical for our own survival.

Incredibly, we have in this new millennium returned to the dark days when talks of pre-emptive castle strikes were in vogue. Are we perhaps closer today to a nuclear holocaust than we were almost five decades ago? Even accidents can happen. Chilling thoughts indeed.

Lessons Learned:

We can destroy the planet.

We just may.

Korean War Monument, Washington, DC.

Chapter 18
Be A Teacher?

By 1958 Americans were again truly gut tired of war and seemingly just wanted to get on with something else. Wars exhaust nations and their people, except in parts of the Middle East, where they seemingly thrive on a steady diet of killing. By the sixties those Americans concerned over nuclear weapons felt they could breathe a little easier. Home bomb shelters were refurbished as recreation rooms with Ping Pong tables.

Idyllic as the concept of peace was becoming, however, activities in Southeast Asia had taken a turn for the worst. Since America had not decisively won the Korean conflict, it certainly shouldn't have been a surprise what was to happen a few years later in Vietnam. The groundwork had been laid; America was no longer considered invincible in the WW II sense. Perhaps the world at large had finally come face to face with the fact that, thanks to means of mass destruction, worldwide wars had become obsolete. However, this seemed to encourage more localized struggles. People have to fight somewhere.

Personally my years in the Air Force had been rewarding, but coming home to civilian life was not all that easy. I had developed limited skills and a certain kind of rigid, narrow mindset from five years in the military. Preparing a resume based on being a nuclear weapons officer, hell bent on blowing up the globe, but not allowed to say much about the classified job activities, resulted in a useless document for obtaining civilian employment.

The Askovian immigrant community had been supportive of its military, but twenty years of war had drained much of their ardor for conflict. Rutabaga farming was always an option for returning Askovian servicemen. Few took the bait, or rather the hoe, however, and instead drifted elsewhere. This devoted mainly Danish immigrant community was now aging and could provide few non-farming opportunities. Realistically, but sadly, the rutabaga had lost its luster as a gourmet dish.

Fortunately I had spent much of my military life studying physics and mathematics, subjects that I had always found interesting and now discovered to be an asset. I headed back to the University of Minnesota with a generous GI bill and a lingering desire to be a teacher, even if I had to take all those perceived mindless mandated education courses.

Interestingly enough, after my nuke bomb-making experiences, the U of M education courses didn't seem all that bad. Some were even outstanding; amazing what aging can do. The ENIAC computer's successors had found their way onto the campus, and so I finally got introduced to *the* computer.

This singular device was an incredibly huge machine with lots of tubes and flashing lights that lived in an air-conditioned room. All programming began first by converting base ten numerals into base two, since digital computers operate on the binary system. The courses designed to teach us to use the computer centered mainly on logic, which I found interesting and challenging. Logic should be a required course for every student and taught earlier.

Enthusiasm was resurfacing on campus after the pervasive nuclear weapon gloom and the end of Korean struggles. The sciences were emerging as the most exciting careers for the future. Medicine, law, and engineering dominated; but there was also renewed interest in the field of education. These were indeed giddy times for academia as the Higher Ed biz turned definitely bullish.

To become a teacher – maybe.

The universities of this time were "feeling their oats" spurred on by optimism and generous government grants. Drug usage, other than booze and smokes, was still around the corner. The psychologists thought they were about to unravel the human mind with their I.Q, Rorschach and Miller Analogy tests—same damn ones used in the service, and equally useless. Supposedly these tests would determine who should be a teacher in the first place, and then divulge how teachers could improve their skills, just like the earlier futile military tests to find officers.

Fortunately, there was still a strong belief that a teacher needed to know some content material before taking over a classroom. Good idea. But this meant taking courses designed to provide a content base, i.e., more classroom hours in math and the sciences.

Historically American teachers have come from

middle to lower class families, again often the kids of immigrants. Becoming a teacher was definitely a step up the economic and social ladder. The value system of the American immigrant and many teachers of that time were consequently similar: study and hard work. Still, there was a nagging concern that maybe teaching didn't have the pizzazz of being a neurosurgeon.

People should probably only go into teaching after they have lived awhile and experienced other things. On my return, I found that time had brought some changes to the College of Education; for surely I had not changed that much. I ended up taking a course from the famous Professor Donovan Johnson, who through the years has also become one of my best friends. He announced at the end of his course one night that the Lab School needed someone to work in the Audio Visual Department. The job paid minimum wages, but had flexible hours.

I got my first paying education job in an area I knew absolutely nothing about. The position was to supervise the use of cameras, projectors, video cameras, and dark rooms. Let your imagination freely swirl around the image of eager hormone laden teenagers supposedly developing film in a darkroom. This A-V job was a hoot.

This was also an exciting time—the beginning of educational technology. The U of M was funded in one of the first experimental uses of television for instructional purposes. The equipment consisted of huge, awkward image orthicon video cameras that consumed megawatts of electricity and constantly needed adjustments, requiring endless hours and lots of federal funds. I found working as a part-time cameraman a valuable experience, in that you are forced to follow the stream of information from the instructor to hopefully the student.

After knocking off the required courses, I was eventually assigned to student teach in secondary mathematics. This experience was the really big nut everyone was required to complete in order to get certified – still is.

My master teacher was more interested in university athletics than mathematics. When I walked into his second-year algebra class, he asked my name, then told me what page the class was on and to please bring him the students' grades at the end of the quarter. I had a great time and got a glowing evaluation. Thank you very much!

The second assignment was a senior consumer math class. This was a fun bunch of restless adolescents, mainly males, whose arms easily reached the floor when they stood up and who thought consumer mathematics was another way of saying "party time." This was the required senior math course for students who had been behind the door when basic number sense was handed out. I had a hell of a time getting this bunch under control; how this eventually happened was serendipitous, but taught me a most valuable lesson.

There was in this class a giant mutant by the name of Jim who had no concept of how many fingers he had, even on one hand. He was a trial every single day, and only because of my good Askovian family upbringing, military discipline, and no guts to take on a big kid, did I fail to kill him. This kid was about as conniving a person as one could imagine, but my gawd, he was big and strong.

Something just had to be done. The situation had deteriorated to the point where it was Jim or me, and no one was betting on me. So one afternoon I called Jim in after school to chew his butt out in no uncertain military terms, just as I had been after loosing an atom bomb years earlier. I was seated in my swivel chair behind a gray metal desk, and he was standing loosely at attention in front of the desk. I began using my best verbal venom as to how I was planning to restructure his unacceptable behavior in consumer math. In this monologue I said many things about his abysmal record, both academically and socially. I was on a roll to verbally destroy this punk.

Suddenly a tear ran down one of Jim's cheeks. This caught me totally off guard, and I asked concernedly, "What is the matter, Jim?"

He replied, "Mr. Hansen, you don't know what it's like to go through twelve years of school and never get a grade above a C, and that was a gift in a shop class."

For sure Jim was right; I did not know. Now what to do? I told him to sit in my chair and I would stand up. I could not believe the metamorphosis that took place when we switched positions. The kid unloaded and displayed a heart big as all outdoors. He had had a tough life and was by no means a dummy.

When we were finished, Jim, now gaining a little confidence, said to me, "Mr. Hansen, if ever anyone in consumer math gives you a bad time, just give me the high sign, and I will take care of the problem after class."

The son of a bitch literally volunteered to beat up any student that I designated as needing some attitude adjustment! I had become a mafia godfather in consumer math; Jim became my consumer math enforcer. Never again was there a behavior problem. I had learned my first really important lesson in becoming a teacher:

Students run the class, not the instructor.

Jim never did figure out how many fingers or toes God had given him, but my consumer math class now ran like a fine Swiss watch. (This was before digitals.) Jim had assumed the responsibility of ensuring that I no longer had to be bothered with discipline problems. Since then I have advised my student teachers that successful teaching is all about how teachers delegate power to their students

Jim taught me the best lesson I have ever learned from anyone about teaching, including a world of erudite professors. That simple underlying lesson was and remains: Teachers can never really know what it is like to be one of their students. If you are sincere enough, however, it may be possible to get them to tell you what their problem really is. Once they know that you wish to help them, they become your warriors.

The term *"boundary layer people"* also applies to our classroom teachers. Just like first generation Americans, who negotiate their immigrant parent's past with the new world order, teachers have the challenge to take societies established tenets and pass them on to America's youth. Tough job.

Student teaching was lots of fun and provided by far the best instruction for entering the classroom arena. Finally, with teaching credentials in mathematics, physics, and chemistry, it seemed time to get out of the academic cocoon and go to work somewhere. But . . . wait a minute!

During this time we were blessed with two daughters, Anne and Kathy. They were healthy, lively, and bundles of joy. They came to life under much different circumstances than their older brother. Times were good, the future bright and exciting.

At the U interesting discussions were going on about the overall future of education in America. The "brain drain" of scholars from many nations was now making enormous contributions to American science. First it had been the nuclear scientists; now it was the rocket scientists' turn to be in the spotlight. The moon needed to have human visitors, declared President Kennedy. America was again in a race with Russia, this time to conquer space, or at least get to the moon.

Having always envied university professors in their work, I felt a desire to maybe, just maybe, see about getting one of them cushy jobs. While working as a teaching assistant and on occasion playing cards with these self-proclaimed mental giants, it seemed as if we all put our pants on the same way, one leg at a time. Somehow they had gotten advanced degrees and were now enjoying the good life. Thus I began tiptoeing into the murky waters of dreaming about getting one of them PhDs. Why not? What the hell, with still some GI Bill money left, teaching half time to feed a growing family, and living in a Quonset hut in University Village with good student neighbors, the dream evolved into a hope.

Back I went to the great Professor Donovan Johnson and asked if he thought I could qualify for a Master's degree. Now as you might suspect, Dr. Johnson is a great professor with keen insight in identifying potential talent. Taking pity on me he agreed to accept me as a candidate for the MA degree. It meant more books and working more problems, but guardedly I was moving in the direction of becoming "one of them."

Surprise! I discovered that graduate courses were a heck of a lot easier than undergraduate. This is still true; professors will connive every which way to teach at the graduate level. Why? The professors know that their graduate students have been exposed to all, and picked up most, of what the senior faculty has to offer. Professors thus become vulnerable and begin to curry the adoration of their graduates. This is best done by writing papers together. If your student should discover something important or do something really great, it is always comforting to be able to say, "I was his teacher," as if the accomplishments were somehow due to you. Hence, graduate students and their advisors often become good buddies—all around a pretty good scheme for the system.

It is a club: The University Club.

After the MA and considerably more nervous, it was again time to approach the great master, Dr. Johnson, to discuss Ph.D. possibilities.

"Let us see how you do," was his simple reply.

Wow, not a simple rejection like, "Where did you get that cockamamie idea?" No, instead with a grin—he grins a lot—I was given a shot at the big one. Of course, nothing is ever guaranteed in graduate school.

There has always been some debate about the difference between training and education. The distinction was never very clear in my mind until one day when I was short on cash. The example that follows is excessive, but it does illustrate how the two words can differ.

The GI Bill was about to run dry, so I needed to find a way to get some cash. Around a university campus there are always sales companies looking for cheap labor. Rusty-Craft Cook Ware (name altered to protect the not-so-innocent), a farm club for the devil, was recruiting sales people. You talk about a greasy job—no pun—this was it, but it enticingly offered quick cash.

I was so naive that I thought all you had to do was show people shiny pots and pans, and they would happily buy them. No, no! First you have to be trained! I figured this would be a great opportunity to be exposed to training as opposed to education—as some contend there is a difference. At these training sessions they had pre-prepared obnoxious testimonials and pep songs that we had to memorize and sing enthusiastically. The theory was that the way you learned this business was by first listening to some pompous hyenas, then singing rah-rah pot and pan songs (yes, they did have them), and finally accompanying "experienced sales staff" to see how sales are done. Interesting it wasn't, but embarrassing it was.

This company of entrepreneurial devils was, not so cleverly, getting the names of new female high school graduates from the farms who had moved to Minneapolis to seek their fortune, or at least get a paying job, with matrimony as the ultimate goal. Most were damn poor innocent farm girls living on sub-minimum wages. The Rusty-Craft trained sales people were telling them life would be forever beautiful if they would only buy a $450 set of Rusty-Craft pots and pans.

The rascal with whom I understudied would brazenly push his way into the one-room hovels of these poor women, throw a beautiful white tablecloth on their dirty floor, and then begin telling these hapless kids that if they could only learn to cook with waterless Rusty-Craft pots and serve a good wholesome meal, rich and handsome men would be crawling at their feet. It should have been funny, but it was tragic.

The salesman required fifty bucks in cash on the spot, and the rest the buyer would pay on an installment plan with the company. The fifty went right into the salesperson's pocket, plus later they got a percentage of the payments if the duped customers continued making their installment payments. The pots were probably worth ten bucks and change before they rusted.

My lead instructor during the "intensive" training period was absolutely a master at extracting money from these kids. He never mentioned that only after the entire $450 was paid did they get the pots!

On one occasion the naive victim, who had just that day moved into her shabby room, didn't have the fifty dollars needed for a down payment. Not to worry. The salesman told her to walk around the apartment building asking tenants to loan her some money. This poor, trusting but brainless soul took off, leaving us in her apartment, and after fifteen minutes returned with fifty dollars, in assorted amounts that she had borrowed from still unknown but compassionate tenants.

After this experience the concept of sales training took a turn to the south in my mind—better to get back to the business of education.

There really is a distinct difference between pot and pan sales training and higher education.

The GI Bill was exhausted; simultaneously the U of M generously awarded me a doctoral degree and suggested it was time to get to work. It was for me a sad occasion! Graduate school had been a vibrant and uplifting experience, especially when contrasted with the nuclear armament.

I got my first college job at the State University of New York in Oneonta, NY. Oneonta was a gorgeous campus, especially in the fall when the leaves blazed in brilliant red, orange, and yellow colors. Most of the students came from NYC and were thrilled to be living on a woody campus in a small town. Indeed an idyllic college atmosphere.

Meanwhile, problems were brewing in Southeast Asia.

Lesson Learned:

Teaching is a fantastic profession.

Chapter 19
Cal State U –
Northridge

The State of California had adopted a three-tier approach to post-secondary education. The University of California would accept the top eighth of its high school graduates; the top third could apply to the California State University System, with the remaining two-thirds having open access to community colleges. Transferability was facilitated based on enrollments and grades. In the 1960s this arrangement seemed like a reasonable idea, although some viewed it as discriminatory.

Comfortable as Oneonta had become, the idea of heading westward to California held strong appeal. I am always amazed at the draw California had and still has on most people; it exemplifies the Wild West spirit, the get-rich Gold Rush, Hollywood, oceans with surfers, gigantic sequoia redwoods, majestic mountains and vast deserts. The state's canal system for moving water from the north to the south is a construction marvel. In the sixties southern California was becoming the center for the aerospace industry. At night Rocketdyne would suddenly shock the valley as they tested rocket engines designed for future space flight. Their roar would reverberate throughout the entire San Fernando Valley. Kids loved this experience.

San Fernando Valley State College was five years old in 1963; it had few academic or historical traditions, and boasted of an eager young faculty, seemingly endless supply of students, and strong state support. The campus was located in the middle of an orange grove in the heart of the San Fernando Valley, merely thirty minutes from downtown Los Angeles.

Our family of five decided to make the San Fernando Valley our home, just as the WW II song had encouraged. Shortly after our arrival a second son, Mark, enriched our lives; again the birth of one of my children coincided with global conditions in which the threat of nuclear war was seen as a possibility for ending the Asian conflict.

The Los Angeles Unified school system proved excellent for our four kids, in spite of its large size; however, large segments of the school population were poorly served. At this time there was no bussing. Schools were divided into three levels: elementary, junior high, and senior high. The teaching and administrative staffs were wonderful.

Fast forward. SFVSC was to become California State University, Northridge, under then-Governor Ronald Reagan. Many of us did not appreciate this name change, which did not reflect the college's geographical and historical affiliations, thereby losing much of the rich Hispanic culture that accompanied the name San Fernando. By contrast, Northridge, neither north nor a ridge, was at that time merely a small, lackluster suburban post office. Located smack dab in the middle of a vast and very flat plain the name is a joke – just like Plentywood, where I had been born. It is indeed sad that CSUN, which was destined to become one of America's prestigious universities, relinquished its founding name that had identified it with a well-known past, an incredible science frontier (Rocketdyne, Atomics International, Skunk Works, etc.), and the emerging entertainment industry. Oh well —

Nonetheless, the campus has grown until today it is the third largest in the CSU system with thirty plus thousand matriculated students. In addition its College of Extended Learning provides adult instruction to almost as many people worldwide.

The Vietnam War was rightfully not popular with most college students, as well as many faculty, during the nineteen sixties and early seventies. Those of us who were recent graduates of the Korean police action, and still subject to recall, found it difficult to counsel students. Tensions throughout the world had not abated; indeed, issues seemed to be growing more convoluted as many nations sought to establish their own identity.

As we watched events unfold nightly on TV, we could clearly see that the doubletalk coming from McNamara and his buddies was not believable. Body-bag statistics were hard to explain to kids. I remember one night my older son, Alex, wanting to know if somebody's daddy was in those bags lying motionless on the boiling hot tarmacs throughout Vietnam. As a father that was a hard question to say "yes" to.

Cuba, the Kennedy and King assassinations, the Watts riots, and Watergate, occurring in rapid succession, left many college students feeling cynical, even hostile, towards America. The shooting of a student protester on the Kent State campus became a cause célèbre. Adults experienced a queasy feeling that no one was in charge, except police who tried to keep some kind of order. The immigrants' dream of a peaceful America was becoming a nightmare. Blissful isolation was eclipsing.

For many students drugs became a sought-after relief, as well as an exciting diversion from reality. The prevalence of recreational drug taking was a forerunner of today's ready acceptance of ingesting chemicals when you don't feel well. Unfortunately, instead of trying to remedy our kids' problems at the early stages, via education and rehabilitation, society, partially through fear, anger and lack of vision turned to incarceration and punishment.

This confused and stressful period of our history did immeasurable damage to America's collective psyche. The government had run amok in trying to convince its citizenry, albeit through lying, that winning a war in a country, far away, of little threat to democracy was in our best interest. A frustrated home front reacted through a wide range of discrepant behaviors, due in large measure to our youth's unwillingness to accept lies from our elected officials, who seemed clueless and callused

Teaching in this environment was a challenge. Students begged to debate the war issue. New departments were formed to focus on civil liberties and women's rights. This academic expansionism created a plethora of new committees and additional layers of administration.

Time flew by as America was undergoing not one revolution, but many. With Richard Nixon as president, we always felt a lingering fear that he would end Vietnam (and the rest of us) in a nuclear fireball, while simultaneously selling us a used car.

To squelch antiwar talk, racism, drug use, and the like, many frightened groups sought to use police force and pass restrictive laws. The result was an almost blatant disregard for authority by many of America's youth. The "Helter Skelter" murders were indicative of the craziness of the times. This trend to use police power instead of education and rehabilitation has unfortunately remained the norm since this period. The number of people in California jails attests to the failure of this approach. We have even made it game-like, three strikes and you are out.

Now that these legalistic approaches to solve humankind's problems have become so much an integral part of our political and criminal infrastructure, even open and unbiased discussions on alternate approaches, including legalization of some drugs, have become virtually impossible. America took a dreadfully wrong turn on many of these issues during the turbulent sixties and early seventies. Education was never given a fair chance to help solve the problems; instead more jails ruled the day, until now the prison population and related costs rival that of higher education.

What in hell had gone wrong?

On a personal level the marriage begun while Eleanor was in nurses training and I was in the military and had also fallen apart. Divorce was not something that immigrants and their kids took lightly; but since our relationship ended we have been fortunate in hopefully minimizing the negative effects on the kids.

While working on a Federal project I met Dixie Lee, whose marriage with two children, Leesa and Erich, had also been dissolved. Though the relationship did not produce a *Brady Bunch* sitcom, it has worked wonderfully well. After living together in sin for years, we were married and are very proud of our blended family, including three grandsons.

At this time CSUN was slowly beginning to assimilate minority students, many of who were immigrants' kids. In this group I found many kindred souls with whom to share experiences. They seemed to have a sense of eagerness along with humor and balance that I believe is characteristic of first generation kids.

Our neighbor in Chatsworth was a family of Vietnamese "boat people". These poor immigrant parents worked round the clock to provide an American education for their children, who all excelled through college. Their kids spoke Vietnamese at home and perfect English in school. They did not want any bilingual educational programs.

Life at CSUN was becoming more satisfying as the war in Asia mercifully ceased and classes began returning to normal. University life met all the earlier perceived dreams I had had of the academic world. Even the regularly scheduled and often boring meetings began to have an modicum of interest, often punctuated by humor, as they often took on an aura of a social events.

But Askovian Viking blood is restless blood, and fun as teaching had become, it was time to expand. Extension—the kind of nontraditional education that had first touched me when my father took me to a U of M course on artificial insemination back in the early forties—beckoned.

Extension—extended university courses offered beyond the standard degree programs, primarily to working adults—is a major component of American education that is seldom given its fair recognition. The range of courses offered is limitless; topics my be broad or content specific. Schedules are flexible to meet the needs of students. Short of exotic advanced graduate courses, extension provides perhaps the most exciting courses offered by any university.

James O'Donnell, a huge balding Irishman, was then the Extension Dean. He had never been outside the country until he joined the Scandinavian Study Tours. Boy oh boy, did he take to international travel/study. He was a historian by training and adventuresome by nature, which provided all the necessary ingredients for expanding the CSUN's extension programs internationally. Luck was again smiling on me.

The overseas courses were primarily for teachers, who constantly need to accrue credits to maintain their teaching credentials. At one time CSUN had courses in some twenty countries. Summer technology conferences and special science programs in Singapore, Spain, Hawaii, Midway, Brazil, and other exotic places, grew from these efforts to meet a variety of needs. Today the offerings also include online and open university programming. To ensure quality of instruction, visits to evaluate overseas school programs were essential—right? Job related challenges.

Developing nations do admire and constantly seek American education; they want desperately to learn English and have the same opportunities as most American kids. Here at home, however, many excellent educational opportunities are too often squandered. We do not appreciate the truly great educational benefits that are available, particularly in the area of university extension programs.

Some years ago in Taipei I met a young man by the name of Peter. His home was a straw mattress behind the elevator shaft on the eighth floor in the Hilton Hotel. One day he asked me if I would help him in pronouncing some English words. His dream was to become an American. He was a motivated learner and became a friend during my short visit.

Several years later I tried to find Peter in the Taipei Hilton and was told he was in the front office. At the front desk I asked for him, and he emerged beaming, dressed to the nines in a dark suit. "May I help you, Dr. Hansen?" he asked.

"Peter, what is this?" I asked in disbelief.

That night he took me out on the town in Taipei and while sharing ideas he said something I will never forget.

"If the same percentage of Americans work as hard as the same percentage of Chinese, we will overwhelm you, because of our numbers," Peter explained. "But I still want to come and live in America. Will you adopt me?"

It is this powerful dream and attraction that drives so many of the best people in other countries to America's shores. We must not lose this attraction.

Lesson Learned:

The best jobs in the world are teaching at any and all levels..

Chapter 20
Teaching
Mathematics

Most teaching positions require that the professor should specialize in a subject area near and dear to his or her heart. Mathematics, allied sciences, and the pedagogy associated with them made a good combination for me. In some ways they complemented my former rutabaga hoeing and nuclear military experiences. Academia had become a whole new life style. It did fit nicely with my immigrant parent's dreams and hopes.

Early on I mentioned that many Americans love slogans related to historical events, and educators are among the greatest slogan devotees. They unabashedly sport silk-screened T-shirts that expound the wisdom of the ages in a nutshell. Often they appear to be whizzing off to an intellectual rendezvous with a Nobel laureate. Since teachers are forever in a hurry, they do need a specialized lingo, and it's all the better if it can be sewn on something to wear—and doesn't cost too much. Any time you put mathematical symbols on apparel, you have a winning product for teachers:

$a^2 + b^2 = c^2$ Pythagoras' great discovery boldly displayed on a T-shirt. What more does anyone really need to know?

Through the years, but especially following WW II, educators have endured and promoted a plethora of educational movements: Inquiry and Discovery Teaching (everybody is a pioneer), Bay Area Writing (as though they write better in the Bay area), Write to Read (play on words), MACOS (political hot potato), Cooperative Learning (cooperate to graduate), and on and on. Educators generate one-liners to quickly illustrate their mission statement long before they think through and define the purpose of the movement they want to begin. It is the American way: Just get going on something and create a slogan. We will figure out what it is all about later.

The Granddaddy Movement — The New Math!

My, oh, my what a fanciful farcical frustrating movement it was, especially for teachers, their students, and parents. This was another classical educational example of well-meaning ideas run amok.

The New Math started off benignly enough. WW II had amply demonstrated that many servicemen did not know a hoe from a quadratic equation. Since many soldiers were the kids of poor immigrant depression farmers and inner city factory workers, this revelation of their meager math skills should not have come as a surprise. Additionally the academies and elite private schools were simply incapable of preparing enough well trained science graduates to meet the war's demands for technically trained soldiers, sailors, and airmen. The result was that instead of hitting the target directly with a single bomb, we would just drop a bunch of them hoping somehow one would hit the target. Cluster bombing.

For example, the famous Norden bombsight might have been an engineering marvel, but it required substantial mathematical skill to use it successfully. Navigation, on the land, in the air, and on the water, depended on the sextant and required a substantial amount of mathematical acumen, including algebra and trigonometry, which many schools were not then, nor are they now, teaching.

Before Global Positioning Satellites (GPS), flyers frequently had to find a plane's location by using a sextant along with some mathematics, all the while being shot at by enemy planes and from the ground. By contrast today's pilots only have to watch a video screen that determines location and when to shoot. But they go faster.

Throughout the Second World War it was abundantly apparent that America had a severe shortage of mathematically trained people, with perhaps one notable exception, the ability to crack military codes. Following the war politicians and deep educational thinkers began pontificating that America needed to improve the teaching of mathematics, beginning in the lower grades. So far so good. The problem was that no one really knew how to do this; thus there was a vacuum begging to be filled.

Government grants to the rescue. Hee-hee.

Sure enough, forward stepped a bunch of well

meaning mathematicians, covered with chalk dust, who had not seen sunlight, let alone an elementary classroom, for a long time. But they had no problem smelling federal grant money to ostensibly improve mathematics teaching and learning in the public elementary and secondary schools.

The clarion "New Math" slogan was to become a supreme example of what not to do to improve mathematics teaching. This was an expensive, well-intended attempt by out-of-touch university professors with large grants to try to vitalize a subject that was being poorly taught to the point where nearly everyone shunned mathematics.

Guess what? Even after the New Math, kids *still* shun mathematics.

Why?

The movement to improve mathematics teaching took off in the mid-1950s following scholarly symposia and governmental reports. But the movement, like all movements, needed "brand recognition". Sure enough, reporters lived up to their journalistic training and in a heartbeat they coined the expression, The New Math. It stuck, stuck and still sticks.

The gravesites of Euclid, Newton, Descartes, Einstein and their math buddies were reported to have rattled loudly wondering and worrying if they had all been wrong these many centuries. Was the New Math really going to replace all their historical contributions?

The New Math term caught fire immediately, largely through jokes from folks who had successfully been using "old" mathematics to create atomic bombs, rockets, new medical procedures, and the like. Suddenly they, too, began to wonder if they should go back to Algebra I to be retooled.

If there was to be a new math, then surely there was somewhere an old math that was becoming obsolete. Several entrepreneurial university professors (many profs are by nature highly entrepreneurial) immediately took up the challenge to create a "new math" that would ensure American school kids would become math literate, and thus better navigators and bombardiers. These self-proclaimed gurus popped up everywhere, from the mountains to the oceans, from the suburban to the urban, from the grades to graduate school. It is fun to read the National Council of Teachers of Mathematics publications and programs of the new math era.

Oh, the fervor.

Teachers got fired up over the damndest issues. A whole new set of terms, along with a concomitant list of zealous advocates, developed. All the pro-numerals, numerals, and numbers got jumbled up with sets and their intersections. If there weren't any apparent issues, they surely could and would create some. It was a grandiose movement in a subject most people didn't give a rip about.

The New Math began suggesting that numerals, sets and subsets, negative numbers, and the like be introduced in first grade, quickly followed by abstraction after abstraction. The fact that the kids weren't learning to associate numbers with the real world was irrelevant.

The endless overlapping circles and other geometric figures kids drew to supposedly discover intersections were infinite in number. Kids quickly began equating infinity with the figure eight on its side. Not to be satisfied with drawing overlapping figures, makers of educational aids were cleverly creating and marketing blocks of beautifully painted wood and plastic for schools and parents to use to show the same thing.

Parents were upset, but too befuddled to do anything. Teachers did not know what had hit their math curriculum. Administrators and boards of education felt the heat to buy new books and manipulative stuff. Publishers could not sign up authors fast enough to prepare new textbooks and tests. The New Math had assumed a robust life of its own and danced merrily on. For some the dance still goes on.

Soon other curriculum areas felt the need to change. Wow—these government grants were terrific. Education was catching everyone's attention, and was certainly not overlooked by those seeking elective office.

It was a golden era for those of us who were able to give talks on these topics and write books about it. The mathematics playing field, i.e., classrooms, began changing rapidly as grants became available to "Implement the New Math". Research projects supposedly were proving the efficacy of this and that, whatever this and that was. It was just great to be a part of this enthusiastic, though somewhat misguided, movement. In its favor, the new math did liven up mathematics teaching in a manner that firkins and pecks had never done in the past.

For the first time four-color printing of mathematics textbooks became cost effective (at least from the publishers' point of view). Initially this process had some flaws, aside from the books weighing a ton. In

Burbank, California a few kids discovered that because color printing required very slick paper, it was possible to erase letters and numbers on the pages with an ordinary pencil eraser. The state, which at that time printed its own textbooks, had to redesign its printing process.

Printing progress—thanks to creative kids and the new math.

Somewhat later a more successful math movement arose that centered on "math labs", wherein kids finally became actively engaged in mathematically centered topics. This was the work of people like Donovan Johnson, Sheila Berman, and others, who had not lost sight of the fact that kids come before abstract mathematics.

Now, decades later, we are beginning to see the results of the new math. Kids are still doing poorly, parents who got totally frustrated during the movement have learned to leave mathematics alone, and more developmental math courses are now needed at the universities. The scientists who do use math, old and new, to solve real world problems are doing splendidly, indeed creating a lot of truly new mathematics. But in all the little red schoolhouses, we still have a long way to go.

It is prudent to study this movement; otherwise we are doomed to make similar mistakes. It began with well meaning educators trying to improve a very important segment of knowledge. The problem was simply that the proponents of the new math didn't take the time to think through the issues about who were the end users. Hell, no; get the grant money while it is available.

Society depends upon teachers to provide leadership—indeed, they get paid for it—but there is a wide chasm between practicing classroom teachers, with all their restrictions, and the "ivory towered" thinkers, who have few restrictions and too often little experience with kids. One method successfully used by the new math zealots to overcome this divide was to provide teachers with summer workshops with stipends. Finally the classroom teachers and the professors were able to work together.

Like everything, you can only stay fired up about an issue for so long; then it is on to something else. Along came another mathematics attention getting buzzword: "problem solving". Yes, by golly, kids have got to solve problems. Who can be against that? Get out and write some more grants for teaching problem-solving.

The problem with the problem-solving fad was the problems.

There remains throughout much of education a challenge to devise learning experiences that are both relevant to the student and simultaneously provide for a future knowledge base that is appropriate for society.

Being a high school graduate of the Askovian Hans Christian Andersen unified school system, I had often heard and enjoyed HCA's story, "The Emperor's New Clothes." This tale describes a self-satisfied emperor whose tailors (easily) dupe him into believing they have sewn him a suit so fine that ordinary people cannot appreciate it. One day he struts down the street wearing this non-garment, and some kid loudly yells, "The emperor is in the buff!" This story has a message for the new math and other educational movements. Lots of it was in the buff. But many were fearful of so stating. Need them grants.

Mathematics through the ages has been one of humankind's strongest tools; it helps solve real world problems in a logical and unbiased manner. It is truly universal, and it continually helps us in our understanding of "the Universe." Mathematics has been developed by people who have needed to solve real problems—growing food, developing commerce, building shelters, curing diseases, making logical arguments, and the like.

Most kids' first exposure to numbers was, and probably still is, through enumerating body parts: how many fingers do you have? Mathematics can be seen as an evolutionary experience, building upon concepts that children acquire, quite naturally, as they mature and become inquisitive.

Mathematics can be experienced and expressed in many ways, from simple counting to multi-dimensional geometries. It is a beautiful and exciting subject, but its appeal is not universal. However, in today's technological world some minimal skills in working with mathematics are essential. This indirectly infers that the curriculum must continually accept change; topics need to be added and others deleted as our world evolves. Herein lies the rub: what to drop?

The new math surely created a climate of confusion and insecurity. But in doing so it also laid the groundwork for additional changes that were to follow. Calculators, followed by computers, were beginning to flow into society. The nerds, the hobbyists, and the electronic whizzes were creating an entirely new order for mathematics applications. Computer languages and codes were quietly being developed until they suddenly burst into the classroom. New math as it had been practiced was now kaput.

Beads on a wire or stick followed by analog slide rules followed by mechanical calculators significantly improved computation, but not until digital computers became readily available did we experience such a sea change in much of our daily use of mathematics. An unresolved question remains regarding today's computer users' basic understanding of the mathematics they now readily apply. Computers have almost instantly removed much of the laborious drudgery that had earlier been part of mathematics teaching. But teachers and schools have varied widely in their attitudes toward computers in the mathematics classrooms.

Guess what we now find? More gurus, with little research to back up their pleas for grant money, expounding upon the glories of the computer in the classroom. This time corporate money is coming from technology interests instead of from book publishers, and they have a hell of a lot more resources, including stocks that everyone likes to buy. Again, what do we do?

The challenge to all school curricula is not unsolvable, if we are willing to shift our perspective from what was problematic at one time in history, to the problems we are we are facing in today's world. Society must help schools develop curricula that will clearly focus attentions on problems of the present and the future. It must be a joint effort, one in which the interests of the students and the future of humanity are the primary concern. This will naturally put the tree huggers and oil diggers into each other's faces, but at least the issues can be discussed using a ton of mathematics—maybe even some set theory!

I enjoy collecting older math books, with their now-quaint expressions of pecks, firkins, vulgar fractions, aliquot parts, casting out elevens, and so on. An American company published an arithmetic book by John Gough in the 1700s using verse for finding square roots:

First to prepare the square, this do,
Point off the figures two by two.
Beneath the last . . .

Kids were expected to memorize this ditty to extract square roots. They also had one for taking cube roots—should you be interested. The verse is three pages long.

When the new math folks strayed from the kids' reality into the mathematician's private and abstract sandbox, they created a problem for nearly everyone. Since we all perceive mathematics in different ways, it is little wonder that the self-anointed "know-it-all" teachers consistently have high failure rates. They are big on pontificating, but less so on teaching.

Extreme educational practices tend to produce monumental academic flops.

Another hallelujah theme intended to improve education was based on the giddy phrase, "Behavioral Objectives." This movement generated monies for its principal investigators and some of my student mathematics teachers. An educational genius in Southern California had cooked up the idea of making a huge, no infinite, inventory of test items. They were referred to as behavioral objectives, i.e., the things that students should be able to perform at a given grade level. Yeah, okay. You can crank them out by the millions and store them in computers to torture kids for eons.

Many of these items consisted of such minutiae that even adding them all together would not get to you to zero. These "banks" (or tombs) of test items were to be used to measure specifically what a student had learned, so the argument went. The concept yielded beautiful charts of meaningless data. The underlying satanical basis for this concept was that people can be trained like lower animals. The name Skinner quickly comes to mind.

One day at an educational conference, where the behavioral objective presentation seemed to be about counting the number of elephants dancing on the intersection of two pinheads—or something like that—I asked the speaker, after his erudite presentation,

"What is the behavioral objective of life?"

Dead silence throughout the audience, as well as from the speaker. Before he got a handle on what he was going to say, I suggested that, "the behavioral objective of life is death." This certainly seemed to fit what will surely happen to most of us.

Everyone had now turned their heads to the back of the room to see where the question was coming from. The speaker had lost his train of thought (behavioral objective), so I was able to add that, "Perhaps rather than looking at the objective of life as death, it is more important to have a bunch of good experiences getting there."

Process may be as important as the product.

Mathematics for kids must be integrated, especially with the sciences and economics of our day. Since these are also the academic areas that kids can relate to, they will quickly find the topics stimulating, and concurrently discover applications about relevant scientific and societal issues.

Meaningful Mathematics for the masses.

The mathematical skills and knowledge we teach must be for the purpose of attaining significant concepts and conclusions about improving and living a better life. As educators we have both the challenge and opportunity to create exciting learning environments that will ensure satisfactory results, i.e., acceptable test scores, at the end of the classroom experience. This academic journey must not become a nightmare of frustrations and rejections, but rather one of enlightenment and personal satisfactions in understanding our universe a little bit better from a mathematical point of view.

Mathematics is a beautiful and indispensable subject that encourages rigor, understandings and insights about our universe. But perhaps most importantly, mathematics is the catalyst that opens children's minds to imagination, multi-dimensional worlds and predictability of future events. Sporting events would loose their luster if it wasn't for mathematics.

The many cultures, throughout the world and over eons of time, that have contributed to the filed of mathematics are testimony to the universality of the subject.

Mathematics, like other art forms, finds enthusiasts, young and old, everywhere. Unfortunately educators have too often failed to adequately relate this beauty to our students.

Understanding a variety of geometries encourages a wide range of interpretations about what reality may really be like. This in turn liberates the mind to dream freely about the significant issues of our being.

Mathematics provides us with an inner peace, along with challenges and warm reassurances when we have successfully solved a tricky problem. The personal "aha" experience that accompanies a mathematical revelation is a reward by itself. It is thus imperative that children's early experiences in mathematics be successful and not failures. It is these early successes that lead to future confidence in decision making situations.

Mathematics easily lends itself to both solo and group interactions. Mathematicians, astronomers, and the gods that be may indeed have much in common. Let us share this knowledge with our kids dreams. Hope seems to infer closure. Hope approaches being a belief. Hope is the guiding beam in the darkness that constantly lights the way for each of us.

The abilities to dream and hope are each individual's greatest possession. Dreams and hopes define human beings.

Without them we would be mindless robots relentlessly turning out one widget after another. This is precisely why schools must always be sandboxes of dreams and hopes for our children.

Freedom is what immigrants seek, and freedom is what education is all about. Freedom defines America, including freedom from religion.

Our clever technologies are taking us far, but for the most part they are binary devices. But is reality really bits and bytes? Suppose the universe is not binary by design? If so, then we are running down a potentially blind alley. Whatever other options may exist will be discovered by the open, inquiring minds of those who dream and hope.

I have been most fortunate to be affiliated, as a boundary layer person, with the Danish immigrants who came to America about a hundred years ago. It is my most humble contention that the knowledge and attitudes that immigrants bestow on their first generation kids need to be remembered, shared, and revered.

Perhaps it is time to view our aging process as the birthing process of enlightenment into a new frontier, where we will experience even grander vistas of this universe of which we are lucky to be a part. It is a dream – not a plan – yet.

Hell, we don't have many other choices— do we?

There are many other boundary layer folks who should be recognized for their invaluable contributions to America. This book is dedicated to America's immigrants, our teachers and our educational institutions, all of who make a most critical difference in our world. With dreams, hopes, and unfettered educational opportunities, a brighter future is assured for us all.

In summary I hope some issues were raised that pique your curiosity, help you to express appreciation for America's immigrants, and sensitize your feelings for all people throughout the world; but most importantly that you continue to foster and enjoy your innate abilities to freely dream and hope.

Albert Einstien Monument, Washington, DC. Brilliant and Humble.

Chapter 21
Grundtvigian Influence

Everyone who enters the hallowed halls of education, public or private, comes with a trunk full of personal philosophies, experiences, and a desire to make the world a better place to live—as they see it. These personal viewpoints have a profound influence on the effectiveness of the academics they teach, but more importantly upon the attitudes they try to engender in their students. This may be quite significant to America, in that many teachers have come from the ranks of immigrants; thus their point of view might be quite different than the established "American Way".

The educational philosophies and practices brought to America from other nations are worth studying, as they are surreptitiously making changes in our classrooms. The issues run the gamut from politics to economics, and now, most importantly, as well the frightening, - conservative religious influences.

The example to follow comes from Denmark, the culture of many of the people who beautified the Askovian Rock Pile. Comparable contributions of unique ideas can be found in other immigrant clusters throughout America. Through the years they have all contributed and enhanced our nation. My Danish heritage and the notions of a rebellious Dane by the name of N. F. S. Grundtvig (1783-1872) greatly influenced the education I received and later my teaching style which was then passed on to the next generation of teachers.

Before you turn off Grundtvig, it is important to note that he had three wives, fathered his last child at age seventy-seven, and named her Asta Marie Elisabeth, one name from each of his three wives. This alone makes him a gutsy guy.

The specific philosophies espoused by Grundtvig could perhaps only have come from a small, socialized nation where free and open dialogue was encouraged. Across Denmark the Viking mystique is proudly cherished. Catholicism and other religions have been mostly unsuccessful; rather, a fairly liberal Protestant mentality dominates. They have a saying that you go to church at least three times during your life; when you are hatched, matched and dispatched. However the state does pay for and insures that the nation has churches and religious leaders. Christian holidays are observed.

The Danes have had a tolerant approach to lifestyles, accepting most behaviors that do not impact on others—as long as they pay taxes.

Grundtvig's ideas and thoughts were unique and controversial in his time. To reiterate the paraphrased summary of his philosophy mentioned earlier, Grundtvig asserted that we can only begin developing a civilized society by acknowledging that all human beings are first and foremost biological entities, i.e., animals, just like zebras, whales, and billy-goats. Only when our essential animalistic needs have been resolved—eating, resting, reproducing, and the like—does it make much sense to discuss philosophies, politics, and religions. Makes you wonder if well fed chickens, pigs and cows are engaging in cosmological discussions that we just don't understand. Many of the influences that Grundtvig had on the philosophical, religious, and educational practices in Denmark began creeping into the first generation Danish Americans via their immigrant parents. These ideas were then examined and modified by the boundary layer people in a way that satisfied both their parents' feelings and somehow fit into the prevailing American culture.

Some immigrants have come to America sponsored by religious organizations. Since many of them were poor and lacked education, they naturally could be persuaded (or manipulated) to accept a religious point of view as a way of coping with the brutal environmental elements pressing relentlessly against them in this new world. The Danish immigrants wasted little time in coming up with the dancing and the non-dancing categories. The dancing folks stuck close to their hero Grundtvig. The others accepted a much more conservative position.

If one buys into Grundtvig's position of "animal first", you substantially alter many ancillary ideas. For example, if a person steals because he is hungry, should he be fed or punished? Prevailing conservative thought suggests both; throw the thief in the slammer and grudgingly feed him. Grundtvig might suggest that the slammer part of this equation might be modified. Rather, you first feed the culprits and then you educate them to the follies of their ways and provide them with positive opportunities so they do not become expensive social misfits.

Grundtvig and others are credited with helping to found the Danish Folk School movement. (The word *folk* here is generic and refers to all young people.) These schools provided food and thoughtful experiences, as well as an obligation for students to work to maintain themselves and the schools.

Johannes Knudsen, who translated much of Grundtvig's work into English, states in his book *Danish Rebel* that one aspect of Grundtvig's thoughts that, "evoked world curiosity was the remarkable system of popular education, the Danish Folk Schools."

As someone who was subjected from birth to Grundtvig's ideas, songs, and writings—in Danish, since that was home and church language—it was natural to strongly support his position about our world. Keep in mind that the boundary layer folks often look at ideas from their parent's native land somewhat differently. The religiosity component in Gruntvig's writings seemed overly esoteric, even convoluted, to me, but his emphasis on human understanding was clear. He seemingly tried to reconcile, as well as prioritize, the physical and spiritual worlds. Another unique facet of Grundtvig's educational approach centered on pedagogy, with a heavy emphasis on the communal aspect of learning. Grundtvig believed it was more important for students to talk and share ideas than to read books. Interestingly he placed a higher value on classroom dialogue than lectures. A translated quote;

"Enlightenment shall be our goal, even about the blade of grass, but first and last, with the voice of the people, enlightenment about life."

Frequently the instruction in the folk schools was

accompanied by group singing. I have often wondered what his take would be on today's computerized classes. Nordic, as well as Greek, myths played a significant role in the instructional process—the notion of historical and cultural connectedness. Ideas flow and grow together in Gruntvig.

Which pedagogy provides the best education for our kids, computer monitor isolation or communal classroom dialogue and singing—hmmm? What is life's purpose?

As a professional teacher, this boundary layer person has modified what was initially a pure Grundtvigian position and tried to adapt so it would apply in today's America.

The Royal Danish Ministry of Foreign Affairs states in their official booklet on Grundtvig:

"Any form of learning by rote should be banned and great stress laid on the teacher's oral narration and on singing and playing games. The precondition for learning anything was based on the premise that the pupils should first come to like the school and what it could offer them."

Knudsen, et al, founded the Gruntvigian Society at GVC dedicated to studying and preserving the thoughts and ideas of this *Danish Rebel*. The organization failed after a brief period, perhaps partly because it did not focus on Grundtvig's social and education concepts, but instead got mired down on older archaic religious issues. By narrowly focusing on the past they failed to learn from his social visions for the future. In his native

Denmark Grundtvig is better known for his educational thoughts than religious. This is an example of how an idea from another country was doomed because it did not involve boundary layer folks to make the transition and adaptation to America.

A question that constantly confronts America is, how can criminal and abusive behavior best be assuaged and controlled? Supporters of the punitive position suggest more prisons, longer sentences, and for the real baddies, lethal injections. But this position has not had stellar success anywhere, including Saudi Arabia, China, and America.

A more fundamental approach must be discovered as to why these heinous events occur. The loudly heralded, but largely ineffective, punitive efforts are unfortunately applied only after the fact (crime) and thus always come too late to prevent the act.

Grundtvigians simply suggest that society needs to first make certain that the human organism's needs are satisfied, then get on with the socially acceptable behavioral issues. In short, do not let conditions prevail that we know foster criminal behavior. Denmark, in spite of its not-so-nice Viking history, has no death penalty, yet a lower crime rate than most other nations. Why? Perhaps because in Denmark there are very few really hungry people; medical help is available, and housing is provided for those needing this support.

Denmark also happens to be the first established nation to allow women to vote and has for years provided socialized medicine. Supporting these services naturally translates into high taxes, thus making it most difficult for individual citizens to amass obscene wealth. Bill Gates could never happen Denmark – nor Enron.

We know that in California the annual cost per criminal is approximately the same as the cost of going to college. America effectively has the same budget plans for students as for criminals.

Surely Americans can do better!

Another observation follows from taking care of people's basic needs first. America could probably have bought off most of our enemies for a fraction of the cost of the military wars we have waged to subdue them. Why didn't we? Could it be the case that nations only get people to fight over oddball philosophies when their basic needs are not being met? While they are hungry and unhappy, their heads are easily filled with hatred and envy for those in America who seemingly have so much—at least by their standards.

Suppose, just for the fun of it, that instead of pounding million-dollar smart bombs down desert rat holes with expensive stealth bombers, we decided to set up free "Costco" and "Home Depot" shops in the poor nations of the world to assist people in meeting their needs. After the frenzied runs on home improvement stores, we would next open schoolhouses and begin to do some serious teaching and thinking. Sadly, we don't even have discussions over the feasibility of such an approach.

Why?

Because we allow perceived hurt feelings to direct our egos and revenge to dictate American policy.

Pure idiocy.

The popular yuppie statement, "Don't get mad—get even" needs a more adult replacement. Something like, "Learn to prevent."

Instead, here is our current scenario: First we create envy in the world by failing to share; next we give our foes a nasty name; and finally we bomb them into submission. Sadly enough, at some point there just may not be other options. These abhorrent conditions have to be prevented long before we reach another boiling point.

A better world begins with a better education of all children - the immigrant's dream.

A "no-more-war" solution might be completely doable right now, at a relatively modest cost and with minimal loss of human life—but for one single factor - it is now politically incorrect. With a few exceptions it is also impossible because of the religious structures that we humans have somehow concocted through the ages. By golly, we still demand an eye for an eye and a tooth for a tooth. And some would say this is good religion?

And we thought that the myths of more "primitive" societies were wacky! Maybe, just maybe we have not improved on them by a whole lot. Thor's rambunctious thundering activities and the Old Testament accounts of people "slewing" each other are not so far apart, are they?

Children are not born to hate. Just as lyricists Rogers & Hammerstein so hauntingly remind us in their *South Pacific* musical:

"You got to be carefully taught to hate and fear – from year to year."

Proposal: Conduct an experiment in which every kid coming in the front door of a public school is initially fed, cleaned up when necessary, nicely dressed, and given rest if needed, before beginning to teach him or her to read and apply the Pythagorean theorem. In this study no religion would be promulgated, only studied in a historical context. Regardless of the sorrows and grief at home, the school would become a momentary haven for all kids, where for a few hours their thoughts and ideas would be shared and flourish, their hatreds and fears assuaged, their enthusiasm for life reborn, under the guidance of competent teachers. We just might—just might—have a fighting chance to improve the behavior of the human race. Why not give it a try?

Lesson Learned:

We have yet to solve our educational problems – could Gruntvig help? Maybe.

Chapter 22
Educational Gems

In spite of stormy clouds surrounding American education as it is evolving today, there are and have been many sterling successes that are less often recognized because of their uniqueness. The following two widely different educational endeavors offer opportunities to those who support the position that education is our main, perhaps sole, hope for the planet's future. They are in a sense *"Boundary Layer Schools."* The examples are:

- **University Extension programs.** These serve a highly diverse adult population and are destined to be the model for education in the future. Their courses provide immediate and essential educational skills for a rapidly changing world.

- **American overseas schools.** There has evolved since the early 1930's a wide range of schools that provide extraordinary education to Americans and host national students living abroad. They are located in almost every nation; affiliations include the Office of

Overseas Schools of the U.S. State Department, the Department of Defense (DoDD), various religions, and many others under the rubric - independent schools. Their global impact has contributed greatly to America's educational image abroad.

These educational enterprises both began as a response to people seeking an American style education in unusual situations or locations. They have made incredible contributions to our global future, but are seldom formally recognized. It has been my privilege to work in both arenas for many years and to discover that these educators exhibit many of the same robust characteristics that epitomize America's immigrants mentioned earlier. In so many ways, they too, are Boundary Layer People.

Gem 1: Education referred to as extension, or extended studies.

University extension programs are the official outreach functions, sometimes with the title of college, that are now providing, at most large universities, a plethora of educational opportunities, largely to working adults. For the most part they are self-supporting, and thus tend to be highly efficient and cost conscious.

The programs that extensions offer have contributed mightily to America's industrial and agricultural success. Many were started by the land grant colleges as a way to enhance local farming skills by providing evening classes taught by agricultural experts. In comparison to the regular tuition-based degree programs, extensions tend to be quite inexpensive and provide unique opportunities to many who simply do not have the time and/or money to attend college full time. Normally courses have no prerequisites to enroll and attendance is occasionally optional. The students are motivated to learn as they have made a personal investment. In general there is no grading, and the reward for completion is often simply a certificate.

The number of students who are serviced by these extension programs in any given year is enormous. The variety of offerings is determined by need, the content is constantly changing to meet new demands, and the instructors come from every imaginable walk of life.

Why are these programs so successful? Simple answer—these courses meet a very specific need and the instruction tends to be direct and to the point. Perhaps most importantly the classes are scheduled conveniently for people who work, and herein exists an incredible expansion opportunity.

Technology has made it possible for education providers to offer courses online on asynchronous schedules, meaning students can obtain instruction almost anywhere at any time. This is truly revolutionary and is significantly altering the landscape of education for everyone with a desire to learn. Once this mode of delivery becomes truly global, look out.

An entirely different breed of self-motivated learners is rapidly beginning to emerge in academia. Knowledge is now almost free to anyone with a computer. Thus the control of knowledge distribution through traditional classrooms will no longer rest exclusively with the established institutions. People who have historically relied on obtaining a degree for the degree's sake are in for an awakening—their diplomas may no longer ensure careers.

In ancient times only the scribes could read and write; then shamans and religions developed their own private lingo. Finally came Guttenberg, and the reins on knowledge control began to loosen. Today we have the ultimate information revolution via the Internet, whereby almost any and all ideas and concepts are freely accessible. As these phenomena become global we will witness a major academic upheaval.

We are now in a global knowledge war, individually, nationally and internationally.

Already we are witnessing this phenomenon in the technologies. The world is looking to those people who have somehow (even on their own—nerds) obtained the skills and knowledge base needed for performing electronic tasks. A generic degree from even a prestigious institution of higher learning may soon become quite meaningless, if the graduate is incompetent to perform specified tasks or dream up new ideas.

Faking knowledge and skills in technical areas is most difficult – generally impossible.

America and other developed nations are now sending huge amounts of data to developing countries to be manipulated, summarized, and rapidly returned by them—because it is much cheaper. Do we have any idea how many people outside of America now have our personal credit data? I think not.

We are all becoming knowledge transparent; there is no place to hide. You know it or you don't!

A global paradigm shift is currently underway as the entire world population is waking up and beginning to surf this huge ocean called knowledge. The notion that a government or nation can somehow regulate scientific experimentation (e.g., stem cells) is ludicrous. Instead of bombing nations that are making bombs to bomb us, we should be investigating other strategies of cooperation so we can all get out of the bomb-building business and into more productive venues.

As American society (hopefully) becomes more and more disenchanted with mindless entertainment, there is in motion a dramatic shift whereby people seek more education and enjoy acquiring new skills. As the delivery pedagogy becomes increasingly inviting and exciting, it will attract even greater numbers of students. This global educational revolution is still nascent, but it will present many challenging problems for students, educators and society at large.

Those who are unwilling or incapable of availing themselves of these educational opportunities, for whatever reason, will suffer in a variety of ways. If their inability has to do with work-related topics, their efficiency and worth to their employer will be lessened; if it has to do with personal satisfactions, they will be missing opportunities for growth and enrichment; and if it has to do with making career choices or changes, they will be limited in selecting options.

As this educational technology becomes increasingly available, each person becomes the captain of his

or her own academic ship. The onus has shifted; up-
dating our skills becomes our own responsibility and
not somebody else's. Knowing how to learn, where to
get the knowledge, and having the "stick-to-it" desire
will be the operatives for every adult's future academic
enhancements. Many employers have already seized
upon this shift in both their hiring practices and maintenance of staffs.

Colleges of Extension are uniquely poised as the
future leaders in these global endeavors. Their strength
is derived from their uniqueness, flexibility and creativity. They have only begun to realize the expansive future that lies ahead in this technological globalization
of education.

**Gem 2: American educational influences
beyond America.**

There is a significant component of American education that is unfortunately known only by a small number of Americans: the American-style elementary and
high schools that operate outside our borders. One of
the premier organization responsible for shepherding
these overseas schools is the Association for the Ad-
vancement of International Education (AAIE), which
was founded in 1966 to assist in serving American students whose parents were employed overseas by the
American government and/or corporations. The AAIE
was initially an outgrowth of a "school to school" partnership idea designed to provide a viable link between
the overseas school and a successful stateside school.

The American-International schools are now growing almost explosively, to the point where their standards and achievement records rival outstanding state-

side schools. Over time these schools have coalesced into regional organizations that serve a given geographical area, for example, Europe, Asia, the Middle East, the Mediterranean, South America, or Central America. They conduct international meetings and provide support services to their constituents.

These largely private international schools are now world class in academic performance and attract students from the local overseas community they serve. The language of instruction is mainly English; the curriculum is primarily American with both Advanced Placement (AP) and the International Baccalaureate (IB) programs available for qualified students. Often their physical plants are superior to stateside schools.

These schools have quietly had an incalculable influence in the countries in which they are located. They are the flagships for demonstrating the effectiveness of the American open and freedom-loving school system. They have become the envy of the host national schools. Their visibility in the foreign nations in which they are located is both positive and negative. Among the locals there is often envy and a frustrating desire to attend the American school. However these schools also help to perpetuate the dream that many have to someday immigrate to America. The political influences these schools have in perpetuating the American dream varies, but for sure they are visible and serve as a window to our educational practices.

These schools all exemplify America's dedication to educating its youth, even when students are to be schooled in foreign countries. To make this happen was not always easy. Wars, natural disasters, political upheavals and the everyday challenges of living in a foreign nation became routine chores. Their tales of "teaching abroad" are gripping.

Since the inception of these schools, they have produced many American global educational titans; a list naming just a few that are currently active would include: Mannino, Luebke, Miller, McGugan, Cameron, Spillane, Davis, and Bentz, from the US State Department; Brown, Strommen, Morris, Anderson, Stiltner, and Betts in South America; Gaw, Hove, Hansen, Sills, Russell Haas, Abushakra, Dorbis, McGlothlin,and Chojnacki in the Middle East; Greer, Ruberto, Greely from Africa; O'Hale, McKay, Tudor and Middlebrook in Europe; Adams, Lyso, Gross, Krajczar, Nelson, Vehey, Jutras, Horton, Dulac, Shoemaker and Cooper in Asia; Sanchez and Mend in Central America; Cobb, Haddan and Rose in Eastern Europe; Broman, Magagna, Grell, Ulkima, Kirkpatrick, Ferrandino, Ambrose, Smith, Price, Berg, and Marino, from the States. The total number of teachers recruited from the States to teach overseas is in the thousands. These are truly America's educational outreach immigrants to other nations—America's global educational ambassadors.

As outbound immigrants from America, their influence and contributions to the concept of global education are staggering. They continually, quietly and professionally create miniature American colonies that display the best of American education. Unfortunately their valiant efforts are almost unknown and unrecognized by stateside educators.

Students, teachers, and administrators who have in some way participated in these overseas schools have been richly rewarded and are forever changed in their attitude and perspective on multi-cultualism and global education.

Many of these American overseas schools began as a partnership arrangement so established stateside schools could assist the international schools. Now the tables have turned, and the international schools should be assisting stateside schools to more fully appreciate the terms *international* and *globalization.*

Frequently these overseas American educators will return stateside to renew their affiliations and get in tune with what is happening in the States. Many express concern of what they see happening, namely a narrowly focused educational perspective that too often has lost sight of the fact that their graduates will be living in a global community—and they are not being prepared for it.

Now after some thirty years of participating in many programs with the international schools it is my humble conclusion that we should begin to view these overseas schools as sources of inspiration and leadership to improve the quality of instruction in stateside schools. We need their expertise and perspective to help develop a new leadership role in restructuring American stateside schools.

Lessons Learned:

University Extension programs are the educational wave of the future.

American-International (overseas) schools are America's global educational showcases and ambassadors.

Both serve America well.

Chapter 23
Tomorrow's Education

Teaching, more than any other profession, has an incalculable influence on our planet's future. As many parents remain aloof from their kids, American governmental officials flounder over selfish decisions or indecision, industry tycoons wallow in avarice, and established religions are caught supporting a wide range of wacky ideas and behaviors, only our teachers are left to establish and maintain some kind of decorum and order.

This new millennium has begun by getting mired down in a resurgence of religious fervor. Most, if not all great religion began humbly and in general were dedicated to helping people live the best life possible. They were humble, often to the point of naiveté. None of them began with gaudy monuments, cathedrals and an army of managers, all funded from prescribed tithes. What is going on now is frightening. We have powerful and persuasive folks purportedly with pipelines to a wide range of perceived deities that are calling the shots from afar. They are cleverly deceiving a multitude of innocent human beings and in the process setting up intolerable conditions for everyone. The intent of this chapter is to summarize and share some experiences garnered over many decades in public education. The concepts expressed are the consequences of having been raised by immigrants in a period of time when enormous changes took place in America and the world at large. The educational techniques that worked during that time frame are now in need of major modification. We cannot continue to simply pile more stuff on our schools. The school's role in our world is changing and with it the tasks of being a teacher.

America's schools must now focus on teaching attitudes as well as content.

Globalization of economics, politics, and major religions is now a fact. However, globalization of attitudes is still a fuzzy dream. To make that happen we will have to dependent upon all teachers throughout the world. They have become our future leaders.

Teachers through the ages have had a stabilizing effect on society. Their mission is noble, their training humbling, and their work demanding, but rewarding. As long as the separation of church and state is maintained in our public schools, America will survive. But schools now, more than ever, need help to ensure that this separation remains in sync with our Constitution.

Every grouping of immigrants has brought to America a varied and an unusually rich assortment of ideas, music, myths, clothing, foods, and the like that contribute to the educational caldron. Any child coming to school in a hand-me-down foreign dress that is obviously different from her classmates' feels a certain degree of isolation and sometimes becomes the object of ridicule. The ideas and philosophies boundary layer kids have learned from their parents and now must share with their new friends can provoke similar reactions. First generations are often embarrassed or ashamed of this mom and pop heritage, but nevertheless it remains for them to incorporate their legacy into the new order. In accomplishing this assimilation America's public schools have generally been supportive and often in the forefront.

The American education establishment spends enormous sums and employs a wide range of workers at a variety of levels, and as a result strongly influences the labor market. Education becomes the whipping post for every politician, and yet for far too many students education remains a source of unfulfilled dreams and promises.

So—is it just possible that our education and training regimens stemming from home, school, and religions are in some way responsible for our present confused conditions?

We are born with only minimum needs that are basically related to our physical survival. But we also intrinsically seek companionship, humor and warmth; we like to be touched and held; we begin smiling followed by laughing at a very early age; we enjoy playing, including singing and being just plain goofy. These components, too, are essential ingredients of an effective education. They are after all the human qualities.

Education is a most difficult concept to define. Perhaps a simple definition will suffice: Education should be the process of inspiring people, young and old, to dream and create satisfying visions of, and for, themselves while not hurting others. Thus, to learn begins with a dream.

Without a vision there can be no significant educational outcome.

A frustrating factor with today's educational policies is that kids are not given any time—whatsoever—to dream. They experience only a relentless hammering to pass some arbitrary commercialized test to placate egotistical parents, political and industrial greed. The results are that many of our kids' dreams and potential visions are being ignored and subsequently lost in their most formative stages.

Test scores and grades have never correlated well with creativity.

Many of the agencies and institutions that are running (or bankrupting) our schools are rudderless and clueless on a sea teeming with students who have very personal dreams and hopes of a better world. Kids, by nature, tend to be highly idealistic, at least in the lower grades. They react negatively to regimented enslavement that may be heading society into environmental disaster.

Most immigrants have a healthy educational dream for their kids. Immigrants helped create and have remained strong supporters of public education. They fervently believe in education's ability to elevate their offspring. In today's climate, however, many of these stalwarts are becoming disenfranchised.

Why is home schooling often replacing the community classrooms? Why have standards of civil behavior in schools become so confused that mayhem is frequently the result? The litany of "whys" goes on, but of course the questions fail to address any kind of solution. More wailing and hand wringing is fruitless.

Educational norms are constantly evolving, as they should. But let's examine who is in charge of this process. What are the motives that are now creating so much unhappiness with our schools and in the students they graduate? And why is teaching, a process everyone engages in, so often maligned and not attracting more quality people?

The simple answer is that this historically honorable profession has, through neglect, fallen into the clutches of self-serving agencies and profit-driven corporations that do not have the kids' welfare, or that of society, at heart. They envision the school's duty as that of producing more workers to make and consume more gadgets.

Somewhat in desperation many states have embarked on a completely counterproductive "high stakes" testing regimen to somehow allay parents' and the nation's concerns over the issue of producing a well trained work force. Herein we find the devil and his deviousness diligently at work.

America does need a well-trained working force, but to do what? Make more useless widgets while taking away life's precious hours? Dominate the world by savage instruments of war because we do not want to share our wealth? Hammer everyone into becoming a conservative Christian who opposes abortion? These narrowly focused issues become flash points (certainly not points of light) and have now become entwined, complicated, and often repulsive. The result is that lots of folks just give up on social issues and become thoroughly self-centered, catering to their personal whims. What has happened to the arts, music, and play? Worse yet, over half out the adult population neglects to vote.

If education is to begin with a dream and a vision, then, by golly, we need teachers and administrators who themselves practice this, and who can inspire, encourage and promote this behavior in their students. Even though schools are beholden to boards and politicians who may have other, albeit more lowly, agendas, educators must continue to envision and support a future dedicated to helping every person develop to their potential.

Lofty mission statements are only valuable when their visions become actions.

Since teachers are the ones who do most of the teaching in our schools, it is perhaps prudent to take a close look at what are they like, where they come from, and what role they should play in the overall scheme of education. From the perspective of a boundary layer person who became a teacher, please allow me to examine the teacher recruitment and training process that seems to prevail.

Teachers are often: surrogate parents, intermediaries with the law, counselors on personal issues, advisors on health and medical issues that parents won't face, and general confidants. This is a tall order. They define a boundary layer.

Elementary and high school teachers have tended

to come from the middle and lower economic groups; thus they reflect middle class values. State-supported institutions of higher learning produce the bulk of teachers. Generally salaries are mediocre and classroom duties challenging, resulting in a high annual turnover within the profession.

Teachers do have other lucrative job options, especially in the sciences, that often lure them from the classroom to research labs. In spite of their dedication to quality, teachers are often handicapped and compromised by the conditions imposed upon them, e.g, large class size, limited resources, children from dysfunctional families, capricious local standards—the list goes on and on.

- Education is now an unstable and confused profession.

- Teachers are damned if they do and god damned if they don't.

- Incredibly we still find great instructors in our classrooms.

What happens after a person decides teaching will be their career choice? Often they encounter derision from their colleagues who are seeking to join the hoards of lawyers and MBAs. (Interestingly enough, students seeking to be doctors tend to be far more sympathetic, perhaps because they understand the complexity of humans. The medical professions recognize that they delve primarily into physical issues, while teachers are immersed in the totality of life.)

New eager teachers run into a plethora of philosophies and psychologies regarding students in general, as well as the specific characteristics of individuals. Each pedagogical position, stated separately, seems logical and well meaning, but in the aggregate they are overwhelming and often contradictory.

The business surrounding testing and grading has become a quagmire. Grades and test scores are now used to "motivate" entire schools to perform better or be penalized. The most frequent result of this absurd system is that the neediest schools receive the least support, both psychological and financial.

On an individual level, grades can be great motivators for some students, but they can also be devastators for others. Students must honestly know how they are doing compared to what they are capable of, as well as compared to whatever standards of achievement exist. Competition is healthy, and most students can handle it; however, some cannot. The many techniques that teachers have devised through the ages to cope with grading would make an interesting study. To summarize grading (evaluations) from my personal experiences:

- **If you do not know your students, it is easy to grade them.**

- **If you do know your students, it is impossible to grade them.**

- **The only grade that really matters is the grade you give yourself.**

- **Grades can literally destroy people.**

• **No single letter or number can ever describe a human being.**

There is no question that standards have to be established and maintained. But these requirements are more significant in some areas than others. To perform microsurgery requires the absolutely highest standards, but in the performance of less critical skills, perhaps some slack is possible if the teacher feels this is more beneficial for the student. It is always a tough call. A dedicated teacher seldom feels satisfied with grading

Could better solutions be found by allowing teachers greater latitude in the overall decision-making process? Administrators, boards of education, and legislatures have all conspired to control the classrooms. Sometimes this has been successful, but often a mess has resulted. The oft-quoted statement about board members never wanting a teacher to be earning more money than the lowest-paid board member is no joke; it is a pathetic truism.

Community control is necessary, but since most board members come to their board position via a political vote, it is often difficult for professionally dedicated teachers to have much of an influence at the board level, where most of the big decisions are made. Each board member comes with his or her own agenda, too often involving monies—theirs or taxpayers'. If they have teenagers at home, you know exactly what they are going to propose.

The less-than-universally-successful experiments in privatizing public schools seemingly do not offer any clear positive solution to who should and how to run schools. The concept of chartered schools would never have seen the light of day, except for the fact that citizens and public school boards failed.

Teachers have generally had only a marginal effect on boards of governance, partly because faculty has often been too narrowly focus on salaries rather than issues of curricula. If for a brief period of time, teachers would back off their personal revenue issues and pressure boards on matters of content, they might win big. Most members of the governing boards would not readily submit to even a first year algebra or history test and have their scores published in the local papers. Why not?

A statewide test for all board members with the average scores posted would rapidly bring an entirely new approach to school administration in America. Suddenly board members would discover the schools' needs for specialized courses, differential instructional strategies, and the like, not just for the kids, but for the board members themselves.

One supporting illustration. While working with the Beverly Hills Unified School District some years ago when computers were entering the classrooms, it was decided that I would help board members become "computer literate". I suggested we go to the computer lab, but was immediately shot down by a very well known personage serving on the board. He wanted everyone to come to me, one at a time. So individual schedules were made. When the gentleman requesting one-on-one instruction came, I asked him why.

He replied simply, "I have never touched the keyboard of a typewriter, and I am afraid that I would be embarrassed in front of other board members."

You talk about board member ego? In fairness, this business tycoon rapidly learned how to use computers, albeit with two-finger typing, and became the schools' biggest supporter of technology. There is hope.

Every human being is so unique that any attempt to assume one-size education fits all is silly. But this approach is often the one taken by administrators and boards. Teachers with inadequate time and resources to properly assist each child are also forced into this cookie-cutter stance. Under these conditions the curriculum frequently becomes primarily the content of adopted textbooks, commercial computer programs, and similar structured materials. Good as these may be, they do not allow for much individualization of instruction.

What results is that the "powers that be", wanting to develop a work force to perform certain functions, are forced to design specific and limited courses of study. Students who can adequately adapt to this restricted regimen are graduated and become employed. But a large number of students whose uniqueness does not fit the often narrowly established pattern are left with little hope of attaining any meaningful "education".

Squandered human potential must never be tolerated by a free society.

The ridiculous statistics and charts showing that the more education a person acquires the more money she/he will make is pure blasphemy. It serves only to fill the coffers of educational entrepreneurs and demoralize the folks who, for whatever reasons, cannot or do not want to go to school.

The real and only question we should be asking is this:

What satisfactions and happiness does a student's educational experience bring him or her as a human being, regardless of the monies he or she will amass?

If this kind of question were asked more frequently, we would have an entirely different kind of student body in our schools and at the universities.

The operative words for improving our schools are:

- **Inspiration for all.**

- **Variety of content and performance standards.**

- **Individual prescriptions based on needs and abilities.**

- **Action, action, action – just do it – stop talking!**

- **Humor liberally provided.**

- **Flexibility, tolerance and understanding for and of everyone.**

These are the same characteristics that immigrants have brought and continue to bring to our country. Unfortunately our schools have become training camps for a very narrow band of industries at the expense of educating students to live a joyful, productive life with respect and tolerance for all.

The task of restructuring American Education is not going to be easy. But remember, this is a can-do nation.

America must not impede its teachers and the institutions they work in from striving to ensure that all their students get lots of one-on-one help, encouragement, and inspiration, along with a good dose of humor.

If we allow our classrooms to become dungeons of unhappiness and personal frustrations, future graduates will no longer become world leaders for a free world. Behind every expression and behavior teachers use to educate their students lurk their attitudes. These, sometimes fuzzy, attitudes must be examined in light of their implications.

Leadership begets leadership, and it begins in every classroom.

Since its founding America has needed to have all its citizens educated, including legal and illegal immigrants, to the maximum. Every brain that is not developed to its optimum is both a loss for the individual and humanity in general.

The mind is now the global battlefield.

Teachers are our future knowledge warriors.

We all live and learn, but unfortunately we live faster than we learn. The real challenge is to improve conditions for learning so as to match the velocity of our living—while also trying to have fun throughout the journey.

Lessons learned:

It's time to revamp American Education.

Only our teachers can do this.

Chapter 24
Sailing and Soaring

We have visited some of the conditions that today swirl about the Ed biz. The problems that education is facing have evolved over a period of time and to a large extent are due to neglect. Perhaps more important is the failure of our culture to fully comprehend and integrate America's stupendous scientific advances into our attitudes, philosophies and subsequently our educational practices.

There is no status quo (there never was).

Nothing is standing still in the universe except some people's minds.

To overcome mental lethargy and actively participate in the evolving universe requires sustained efforts. A sense of restlessness coupled with unrestricted curiosity is the natural order of things; this produces immigrants and teachers. Whether or not everything is running downhill, as the Second Law of Thermodynamics (entropy) suggests, is moot. What we do know is that everything is in motion. This is exactly the rambunctious spirit the immigrants promulgated when they came to America.

Our western philosophies and religions have, until now, evolved somewhat in parallel with what was known about the universe. The flat earth notion was replaced with a round earth idea; later on, the sun replaced the earth as the center of everything; then our Milky Way galaxy became rather ordinary; now all bets are off as to what is really going on—and is there any end insight?

Each of these events struck a blow to the haughty view that humankind is something really special. Until recently most western religions grudgingly accepted and slowly assimilated these findings. But now, instead of moving forward based on scientific revelations, many folks are hunkering down or even retreating to more primitive times, when I guess things were simpler. Nonetheless, revelations keep cropping up; old ones need to be modified or replaced.

Enlightenment and ethical leadership are the duties and responsibilities of education and educators.

Supposedly a long time ago there was the Big Bang, and everything has been flying apart ever since. Typical fifth grade classroom. Trying to hang on to things as they whiz around, except for a fleeting moment, is ipso facto impossible. The lesson to be learned here is best summarized by the phrase "carpe diem"—seize the moment— it ain't coming around again. America's immigrants have and continue to personify this attitude. Luckily they have also passed this attitude onto subsequent generations.

The process is called teaching. Teaching is inspiring students.

We cannot afford to loose sight of this vision, even as the so-called "golden years" or "the age of final opportunities" approach and roll over each one of us. The universe's movement, regardless of direction, is relentless, and our continued survival depends upon active participation. Perhaps that is another reason we find so many older immigrants still active; they were from the get-go intuitively endowed with a sense of movement.

We began by comparing a certain group of people, the children of immigrants, with the boundary layer phenomena that exist in the physical world, that thin film of molecules that makes it all happen. We can also see boundary layers of other individuals, some who today struggle to infuse newly revealed scientific revelations with older ideas that were based on more limited data. They too, are our teachers.

Ideas and motion cannot exist apart. They are like time and space – inseparable.

I will try to make a case for the interrelations between movement and concepts by examining how exploration, by boat, plane, or spaceship, is accompanied by ideas that are equally mobile.

The Vikings of old were always into boating; hell, it was the only way of getting around to all those islands, as well as away from them. So sailing was instilled in every child at an early age. The Viking boats tended to be sleek and simplistic, one big square sail on a single mast. Where they roamed is still being discov-

ered. Boats were also accepted by Vikings as the vehicle of final departure. The departed was laid out in a
boat that was set on fire, and off they went to their waiting buddies in Valhalla.

Sailing, like flying, carries symbolic meaning beyond being a mere vehicle of locomotion, commerce,
and sport. We understand how the mind "sails away"
or "flies off" as expressions of a profound chord in humankind, our desire to extend ourselves through the
movement of ideas.

Whoever made the first "boat" was expressing that
deeply ingrained human spirit of needing to move on
water. This is probably not a surprising yearning, since
eons ago humans permanently crawled out of the
swamp in need of a suntan. We can observe this fundamental nautical quest in our kids' excited movements
as they eagerly splash with a rubber ducky boat in their
bathtub, swimming pool, or horse tank. The spectacular gambit of one guy's walking on water some two
thousand years ago created quite a stir, but it never
caught on. Seems walking on dirt remains a given by
virtue of being born a primate.

Sailing teaches patience, anticipation, and a steady
hand on the helm, as wave after wave dashes against
the boat's hull while the winds blow in the direction of
low atmospheric pressure. Overreacting to these forces
is counter-productive. Every sailboat is a captive of
design, wind, and water; the helmsman's skill is to ensure that everything works in concert.

It took a long frustrating trek for humanity to
progress from that first sailing vessel to the ability to
soar in the skies. Many obstacles, with accompanying
failures, had to be overcome before final success. However, after the airplane worked, it was a relatively short

historical hop to humanity's successful venture into space.

These are all physical activities that extend the human desire for expanding our movements, as was dictated by the Big Bang. Future travels into space are now primarily monetary challenges. Many of the physical concepts in space travel are well understood, although the time factor remains a hurdle.

But what if the elusive time factor is not the barrier we assume? Wow!

Before leaving sailing and flying, it should be noted that these two activities put human beings in close proximity to the natural order of things. Those who wish to enhance their personal experiences of our physical world would do well to participate in sailing and flying. These physical activities speak to our mental desires to go beyond the present—forever moving onward. Ideas and motion are interwoven.

To obtain the maximum benefits from sailing and flying, you must actually do them, not merely sit in a comfortable overstuffed seat watching movies while drinking martinis, all the while hoping that the helmsman and or pilot knows what he or she is doing. Taking the rudder and steering a small boat while the wind propels you through the water is an incredible extension of basic human capabilities. You directly experience the forces of the wind, rudder, and keel as extensions of your own mental and physical processes. First you mentally visualize where you wish to take your boat, and voila! Your mind and body interact with the natural elements to help you reach your destination— your vision. Sheer magic.

Likewise, steering a course through the air while piloting a small plane, glider, or balloon, you experience an eerie three-dimensional sense of freedom and control. As you gain skills, your mind, arms, and legs feel and know instinctively what to do. The saying "flying by the seat of your pants" is indeed a truism. Your butt is said to be your most sensitive instrument when flying an airplane.

While watching the most elegant of sea birds, the Laysan Albatross, soaring majestically over the Pacific Ocean, one cannot help but feel, or wish, to be part bird. Their uncanny ability to gracefully navigate and reckon time periods is truly a marvel. Just what are the forces in nature that they are in tune with? Can we ever know?

These intriguing thoughts and challenging questions about nature belong to us all; we do not need laboratories or large government grants for mental explorations. Only the freedom of mind is needed. These mental excursions and reveries can easily be abused or destroyed, however, by shortsighted individuals or agencies who feel threatened, so in their insecurity seek to limit and control. Each and every human spirit is both free and fragile. No one has a right to tamper with it, except its owner.

Humankind's next major journeys appear destined to be even more exotic than sailing or flying, even in space. For a brief moment, try to imagine that the human spirit can soar through the dimension of time as well as that of space. The possibilities become mind-boggling.

To participate in this venture, we must first shed lots of old baggage.

Herein lies the rub. We must relinquish the belief that people are the center of anything. We are only a part.

We are ever so slowly learning that we are indeed a part of everything.

If we can accept that fact, then humility and sharing will replace ego and greed. Magically the dream of the utopian Garden of Eden will appear. Time dies.

Future immigrants will be time travelers, where the past shackles of weight, time and distance are jettisoned and replaced by phenomena we do not yet understand. The concept of time, as we measure it, may not even exist. Indeed, the manner in which we now reckon time is at best hokey. Decaying (rotting) atoms is what we now have, but my gosh, this is certainly not an elegant measuring stick.

In a yet-unexplored timeless realm, Newtonian physics may be replaced by forces and energies that will completely overturn existing explanations. The Copernican Revolution, which supplanted the Ptolemaic Theory regarding movements in our solar system, will pale by comparison as the concept of time loses its current restricting control.

From our current level of understanding, we may only be peering in as we stand at the edge of the universe. The so-called "Dark Matter" that is now bugging astronomers is not at all well understood. Some indications are that it may account for as much as 95% of the physical universe, at least as we think we know it. Humankind's feeble attempts to explain phenomena with ideas discovered decades, or even centuries ago, are obviously myopic. Our bubble is much too small.

But wait – there is more.

The ephemeral worlds of the spirits, have seemingly existed from the beginning of time to the present, are undoubtedly still lurking and smiling in the shadows, waiting for humankind's mental evolution to discover their reality. The very fact that they are mentally conceivable, with an occasional rare and unsubstantiated anecdotal account of their existence, gives support and hope to the notion that there may indeed be many other dimensions to our universe.

The mystics of the East, who have been around a long time, have generally been ignored, often even ridiculed by Westerners. Most of us have not taken time to investigate their assertions and behavior. How arrogant.

Today it is the astronomers, the mathematicians, and physicists, joined by the artists, poets, and a few freethinking theologians, who are seriously engaged in multi-dimensional, even mystical, discussions. However, the dreams and hopes for a future without time as a limiting factor belong to everyone.

Facetiously I remind family and friends that when my time comes to move on, the plan is to ascend. This approach is certainly less messy than the method now taken by most. The major concerns about ascension pertain to tax and insurance matters—these issues are not covered in the policy's fine print, nor does the government provide a Secretary for Ascension from whom to get advice.

It is probably true that, if we do not destroy each other first, we will some sunny day understand how to move about in more than three or four timeless dimensions. But as long as our energies are unfortunately focused on more primitive matters, these flights of fantasy are not even seriously considered, except by a few dreamers, nerds, and kooks—which may define most of us.

Exploring these now seemingly eerie realms will be akin to nothing else the human species has ever experienced. It will truly be a quantum leap, the outcomes of which are now completely unimaginable. Our present **gods** are much too small, as C. S. Lewis admonished years ago, but they currently have a stranglehold on their devotees—and they are sure as hell not worth dying over. It is most frustrating that most of our traditional earthly religious establishments, created in periods of time that were totally out of step with today's world, still wield such fear, hatred, and control. Rather than lead in enlightening and encouraging growth, they impede exploration and expansion by wallowing in the past and applying edicts that sprang from less knowledgeable times.

Perspectives do change over time. They are now changing rapidly – but which direction are they going?

Case in point. By all accounts, Christians, Jews, and Muslims (in alphabetical order) all consider Abraham one of their major heroes. Here was a guy, if we can believe the accounts, who was about to skewer and barbeque his son when, thank god, God told him to knock it off. Had this episode taken place today in Central Park, New York, I suggest fewer folks would seek to claim Abraham as their hero. Maybe not. Let us not forget the story about the "Emperor's New Duds".

What have we learned?

Truly, it is sad and grievous that America has been so savagely attacked, but the 9/11 catastrophe must be viewed as a lesson to be learned from and not an occasion to justify bashing the hell out of other, less fortunate people in the name of god—ours or theirs. Isn't it incredible that we now have gods fighting gods, just as in the mythical past? Thor, Odin, and their later buddies in the Old Testament seemingly are still alive and well.

Periods of great stress bring out a variety of odd behavior, as we saw earlier when the Viking immigrants got stuck along the Great Askovian Kettle River. Today we have equally stressful moments, but these events should not be catapulting us back into thinking like the Druids of old.

Gloom and doom are the deadly signs of ignorance, fear, and lack of confidence. Is this retrenchment attitude arising because our educational practices have slipped? Just perhaps.

We can move forward, albeit with lots of sadness and grief, to ensure that a type of Grundtvigian attitude prevails, wherein people's earthly human needs are satisfied, followed by philosophical and social discussions in a less combative environment. We must do everything in our power to somehow dissuade kids from committing suicide-homicide by strapping bombs on their bellies and walking into restaurants in the belief they are doing something wonderful for their religion.

The question has been asked, "Would Grundtvig's open folk school philosophies also include, freedom *from* religion?" If America's educational foundations were free from all religious influences, how might they better educate the next generations? Is it possible that Humankind's common pool of decency toward each other could inaugurate a free and peaceful world with no weapons of mass destruction, if freed from religious prejudice?

Collectively homo sapiens have had a checkered rise from the swamps of time gone by, but the journey has constantly provided deeper insights into the universe at large. This suggests there is hope. It is only now that the species is faced with making creative decisions to avoid our own total annihilation. These critical decisions must not be based on prejudice, arrogance, greed, a profound sense of futility, or worse, that some god is directing the battle from afar and only understood by a few.

Our status in history is similar to that faced by immigrants as they left intolerable conditions to come to America. But our dilemma is that now the only frontier to escape to is space, and we are still a long way from making that an option.

The solution lies in using our talents based on reason and tweaking our attitudes to reflect good will towards all. Our tiny blue boat Earth has never been as stressed as it is today – and it is entirely of our own doing.

Now the really good news is that the "can do" Americans have the ability and necessary skills to go forward.

But do we have the will to change our attitudes?

The haunting question alluded to at the beginning was, to what extent was America partly responsible for the tragedy we sustained on 9/11? An extension of that question has to do with how far might this catastrophe extend.

Chapter 1 began by listing a few traits of the immigrants that have contributed to the greatness of America. It is now time to list a few specific challenges for the future that are essential for global survival and happiness. This "to do" list contains, but not limited to -

- **First and foremost the world must solve the population growth problem. The brutal manner some Asian countries have used to contain this problem is unacceptable, but the problem is solvable with education.**

- **We must restrain unbridled accumulation of wealth by a few individuals, corporations, governments, and religions. Education can effectively teach attitudes of sharing and cooperation.**

- **America became strong based on tolerance of other points of view within America. We must teach and practice tolerance—globally.**

- **The current "Religious World Cup" race must be curtailed in terms of power, money, and influence. Each person has their own unique relationship with** their "maker", but this is private and should not be manipulated by evangelical zealots, who seek to control people for their own greedy and perverse ends.

• Philosophies and religious tenets must evolve to encompass the incredible knowledge that our sciences are uncovering daily about our universe, instead of retreating to primitive shibboleths and myths. Ancient prophecies be damned. What are today's prophecies, based on new knowledge and experiences?

• The possible world of the mystical should be viewed and examined in the same manner as the physical world. The study of multidimensional worlds deserves at the very least a fair hearing.

• Knowledge of the earth's ability to sustain our obsessive consumptive behavior must be altered downward with guidelines and parameters that will ensure our planet's survival. We do not have infinite capacity

• Knowledge must prevail over ignorance, yes; but attitudes should dominate and guide us.

• Greed and avarice, ever present and pervasive, will continue to challenge our survival, but perhaps after recent events American society will, as has happened in Scandinavia, take steps to be more insightful and curb abuses.

- **Aging, by individuals and nations, is perhaps a myth. Avenues of optimism that encourage continued growth and development must replace the sometimes-bumpy roads of longevity.**

- **Great people and great nations lead by vision and compassionate actions, lesser ones by lashing out in revenge like bratty kids.**

Currently America is eminently capable to hammer smaller nations into submission, but horribly weak on its long-term visions for the planet. In order to change this dismal situation, it becomes essential to infuse globally sustaining ideas and attitudes into our educational systems, followed by diligent practices.

We can do it. Yes we can!

America is a nation of immigrants, followed by boundary layer people, who are the truly lucky ones. It is herein that the blending of ideas, experiences, and beliefs from around the world can become an American—indeed a global—reality, and where happiness and bliss may become everlasting, as other unknown dimensions are revealed.

The prospects for an ever-improved existence are exciting, powerful, and best of all probably —*attainable*—but only if we first dream it.

Lessons Learned:

If you can dream it, it just may be possible!

If you can't dream it—it is for sure not possible!

Thoughts on the Future

The thoughts, notions and attitudes expressed herein are dedicated to American immigrants and our teachers who epitomize humankind's desires to be free and knowledgeable about our universe. When you don't have freedom, you can only dream and hope about obtaining it. Dreams precede and beget hope. The immigrants to America arrived with a pocketful of dreams under the brightly shining guiding star of hope. Just as Polaris had earlier led the rambunctious and dreamy Vikings of old to the renowned Askovian Rock Pile, it was the star of hope that, although often beclouded, mentally sustained the Danish pioneers in America.

Dreams (probably) set humans apart from other animals, although we can't be sure. We don't even know where our own dreams come from—though they seemingly keep coming from some mysterious "ether". But without the security blanked called hope, our lofty dreams often fade into sadness and an unfulfilled oblivion.

There are layers of dreams and there are layers of hope.

Dreams can be frivolous, like the ones experienced while lying on the cool earth when you should be hoeing rutabagas, gazing at puffy white clouds as they dance merrily and carefree in an endless deep blue sky. Dreams can also be wishes for a desperately ill child to be healed. Dreams flit about like monarch butterflies in a warm sunny flower patch. Dreams come in a variety of colors as well as in shades of gray. Dreams vary day to day. Dreams are expressions of the "if only" syndrome. Dreams, when they become nightmares, can run amok, producing fear and inciting violence.

Hope tends to be more realistic, stable, and focused. "I hope to pass my driver's test." Hope can also reflect deep desires: "I hope there is an afterlife, and hope to hell it not be hell." Hope is less flighty than dreams. Hope seems to infer closure. Hope approaches being a belief. Hope is the guiding beam in the darkness that constantly lights the way for each of us.

The abilities to dream and hope are each individual's greatest possession. Dreams and hopes define human beings.

Without them we would be mindless robots relentlessly turning out one widget after another. This is precisely why schools must always be sandboxes of dreams and hopes for our children.

Freedom is what immigrants seek, and freedom is what education is all about. Freedom defines America, including freedom from religion.

Our clever technologies are taking us far, but for the most part they are binary devices. But is reality really bits and bytes? Suppose the universe is not binary by design? If so, then we are running down a potentially blind alley. Whatever other options may exist will be discovered by the open, inquiring minds of those who dream and hope.

I have been most fortunate to be affiliated, as a boundary layer person, with the Danish immigrants who came to America about a hundred years ago. It is my most humble contention that the knowledge and attitudes that immigrants bestow on their first generation kids need to be remembered, shared, and revered.

Perhaps it is time to view our aging process as the birthing process of enlightenment into a new frontier, where we will experience even grander vistas of this universe of which we are lucky to be a part. It is a dream – not a plan – yet.

Hell, we don't have many other choices—do we?

There are many other boundary layer folks who should be recognized for their invaluable contributions to America. This book is dedicated to America's immigrants, our teachers and our educational institutions, all of who make a most critical difference in our world. With dreams, hopes, and unfettered educational opportunities, a brighter future is assured for us all.

In summary I hope some issues were raised that pique your curiosity, help you to express appreciation for America's immigrants, and sensitize your feelings for all people throughout the world; but most importantly that you continue to foster and enjoy your innate abilities to freely dream and hope.

Some years ago, Piet Heim, a well known Danish scientist turned poet eloquently reminded us in one of his famous Grooks;

**Mind
These three,
T.T.T.
Hear
Their chime;
Things Take Time!**

So let us be patient and enjoy our sojourn.

Lesson Learned:

Dream and Hope, fellow vagabonds.

Our journey is infinite!

One more time —Skoal!